Bringing Heaven Down to Earth

American University Studies

Series VII
Theology and Religion

Vol. 83

PETER LANG
New York · San Francisco · Bern
Frankfurt am Main · Paris · London

Eric Steven Dale

Bringing Heaven Down to Earth

A Practical Spirituality of Work

PETER LANG
New York · San Francisco · Bern
Frankfurt am Main · Paris · London

Library of Congress Cataloging-in-Publication Data

Dale, Eric Steven
   Bringing heaven down to earth : a practical
spirituality of work / Eric Steven Dale.
      p. cm. − (American university studies. Series VII,
Theology and religion ; vol. 83)
      Includes bibliographical references.
      1. Work−Religious aspects−Christianity.   2. Spiritual
life.   I. Title.   II. Series.
BT738.5.D28   1991   248.8'8−dc20   90-48098
ISBN 0-8204-1518-9   CIP
ISSN 0740-0446

CIP-Titelaufnahme der Deutschen Bibliothek

Dale, Eric Steven:
Bringing heaven down to earth : a practical spirituality of
work / Eric Steven Dale.−New York; Bern; Frankfurt am
Main; Paris: Lang, 1991
   (American university studies : Ser. 7, Theology and
   religion ; Vol. 83)
   ISBN 0-8204-1518-9
NE: American university studies / 07

DEDICATION

My book is dedicated to Reed Henning (saxophonist, Sunday School teacher emeritus, retired painter...play on, Reed!) and all those workers of the world who toil their lives away, often unto death, or nearly so; but who, through the grace of God, come to the realization that the true and most worthy work is the love and worship of God and the love of and service to one's neighbor.

ACKNOWLEDGMENTS

This book has been a long time in the works and I am thankful to many people for their help and encouragement. I want to especially thank Clare Fischer, Sydney Brown, John Coleman, my brother and fellow worker Daniel Dale, my sister Ana Gobledale, the Disciples Divinity House at the University of Chicago, and most of all my wife, Cheri Pierre, for her support in our sharing of a common path of work and spirituality.

TABLE OF CONTENTS

INTRODUCTION:
REFLECTING ON WORK

Writing this book has not been an easy task. There have been highs and lows throughout the process as I have struggled to maintain clarity and continuity. The irony of attempting to write a book on the subject of work and spiritual fulfillment, while struggling myself with a new job and a new working situation, has been both amusing and frustrating. Indeed, endeavors to find a balance between my work and my reflection have proved elusive and fleeting. The balance has been best when disciplined—when I had set hours for writing and I stuck to the purpose of that designated time. The awareness of daily human life—birth, death, struggle, celebration—has a way, however, of taking precedence in a pastor's life over writing, best intentions and discipline notwithstanding.

As I reflect on the different types of jobs I held while working on this topic, I am aware that I have personally experienced the dynamics of which I speak, in particular,the distinct difference between physical and intellectual work, especially as they impinge upon the other parts of a person's life. When you are done with physical work for the day, such as painting or construction, you are finished; it need not concern you any further. Intellectual work, on the other hand, is (almost always) never finished—you carry it with you all day and night and week.

I am also aware that intellectual endeavor, by its very nature, does not necessarily leave the mind free to contemplate in the midst of work; something which physical work does permit. Echoing this sentiment, the Desert Fathers of the early Egyptian monasteries and hermitages, and the writers of *The Philokalia*, among others, add their voices of experience. In light of this perspective, I found myself in the worst situation; as a pastor I am an intellectual worker and I am also trying to reflect or intellectualize on my experience. I was never finished with my work; I was never at rest.

In my ministry, as well as during my painting days, I am aware of many people who do not know or believe that there is a source of grace; that they can have access to a transformational power in their lives. Though I might forget the source of my being during the midst of my daily work, I do attempt to make contact with that source regularly through prayer and meditation. Thereby, I find that I am able to get perspective and to re-center myself.

In striving to find and maintain a balance between my work and my reflection I have a firm conviction which grounds and sustains me. It must be difficult for people who do not have such a grounding and a support to keep on going day after day. Central to my sense of work and vocation is the desire to "turn the world on," that is, to share the hope and meaning I experience in life, and which I believe is God's intention for all people. As such, I am an evangelist; I would proclaim the "good news" of God's love to all people.

Evangelism is for me a practical affair; it has to do with the flesh and blood of peoples' lives. The good news about life is not (it can not be) theoretical. It is not an idea which a person thinks about. The evangel impinges upon a person's life and calls forth a response—a lived response. Such a response affects one's life and thereby changes how one lives; it has practical consequences.

I have named the transforming power present in life "SPIRIT." To reduce a complex theological and philosophical issue to manageable terms, let me simply define a central term for my argument as follows: *spirituality* is that human striving for the transforming power present in life; it is that attraction and movement of the human person toward God, toward the divine.

Spirituality is a popular subject these days; there is a general awareness of and interest in the subject. Yet, I am struck by the apparent unreality of so much of what passes today for spirituality. It seems little has been learned from the long history of human religious strivings, when many "spiritual" writers and proponents continue to limit spirituality to personal prayer, to so-called "spiritual" issues as opposed to "material" issues, and to the church or to the "religious" and "holy." The scope of spirituality must be enlarged. Spirituality must include all of life, not only that which we generally think of as religious. It must include our homes and our jobs as well as our prayers and our churches. Spirituality must be *practical* so that we have ways and means of integrating it in our daily lives.

To say spirituality must be practical, that it needs to speak to us in our daily lives, implies that spirituality is relevant to our *work*, which is precisely at what, and where, we spend the majority of our daily lives.

Work is so mundane. Yet work is all-pervasive. We work all day, or night, and then think of work during our non-working hours. It is often our main topic of conversation; we know our work best, it is what we do, it is what we are good at and knowledgeable about. We identify ourselves by what we do: carpenter, preacher, farmer, teacher, nurse, secretary, foreman, truck driver, musician. We define ourselves by our work.

And yet, how often do we reflect on the purpose and meaning of our work? Of work in general? Beyond the basics of providing income for food and shelter, why do we work? What, if anything, do we get from our work? How does work contribute to our lives as individuals and as a community? Is work ever detrimental to our physical, mental, emotional well-being? And if so, when and why? Is there something "larger" at work when we work?

My position is that there is very definitely some "larger" activity and purpose at work in us and through us when we are working. Going beyond a "theology of work" and also beyond an "ethic of work" I want to speak to the "inner work" possible for individuals in the midst of their daily work and lives. Although I address the meaning and purpose of work and I struggle with the consequences of different types and situations of work, my overriding concern is to articulate how one is to find spiritual fulfillment in everyday life. To accomplish this I draw from the fields of art, worship, economic and social theory, monasticism, and the mystical and spiritual writings of the world's religious traditions.

I hope that this book will serve as a guide for others in devising one's own handbook or guide for daily work: daily work on one's self and daily work on building a more fulfilling human community and world.

1

TOWARD A PRACTICAL SPIRITUALITY:
WORKING OUR LIVES AWAY—
TO WHAT END?

Work is that which most people do most of their waking lives. Yet, there is a conspicuous lack of theological reflection on work. During the past two or three decades this lack has been somewhat remedied, though in a sporadic fashion. Within the broad field of spirituality very little has been written specifically on work. My reflections on work and on spirituality initially arise from my own personal experiences as a worker.

Over the years I have worked as a painter and floor installer, a taxicab driver, a bookstore clerk, a construction worker, and as an ablebodied seaman in the merchant marines (of which I am a retired, full-book member). The life of a worker is not foreign to me. I have experienced the pains and joys of manual labor. I have lived, and do so now, among those who toil daily for their sustenance. I know the sweat and grime, the cussing and frustration, but I also know the camaraderie and celebration, the trust and cooperation that all working people live and breathe.

As a pastor I have been privileged to step out of the working person's life and to view it from a different vantage point. My first ministry position was as an industrial chaplain to the merchant marines and waterfront workers in the San Francisco Bay Area. Of a sudden, I was invited by ship's captains and officers to their cabins and offices, and to their mess (dining room), something which, as a crew member, I had not experienced. Though I was one of them, a seaman, my role as chaplain allowed me to see these men and women and to interact with them in new and different ways. Thus was I able to learn things I had not known, about work and about myself.

My personal searching has led me to the spiritual fonts of the world's religions. Therein I have found much sustenance for life, work, and ministry. Yet, little has addressed my life as a worker and the workplace itself. I have had to construct my own synthesis. This is not to say that I have not found inspirational or appropriate ideas and disciplines, for I have. What I am saying is that very little addresses work or the workplace as the arena for spiritual practice. Most of what I have found is addressed to and for those living the monastic life, which is well and good but leaves a gapping hole, namely, all the rest of us.

The search to construct my own synthesis has become embodied in this book. Part of spirituality is a search; this book is my search, my journey, centered on the issue of spirituality and work.

The contemporary spirituality of work which I am attempting to provide is a way of evaluating the questions I raise for a general re-evaluation of both spirituality and of work. It provides a re-examination of original, and basic, questions. Such a spirituality of work is both new and different. It is not monastic, in that it is not set-apart, nor is it quiet or silent. Yet it draws much from the monastics, as they have reflected on the role of work within spiritual pursuits and the spiritual community. This spirituality seeks to instill an attitude of quietness within the worker in spite of the noise and/or activity in which he or she works.

Three issues need to be addressed in order to construct a practical spirituality of work. First is the need to bring heaven down to earth, where we all live. This is an overriding concern but not so much a tension as the other two issues. Second is the need to heal the split between both contemplation and work and between worship and work, the latter split including the realm of art. And third, there is a need to transcend the false duality between the sacred and the secular, between spirit and matter. Each issue is the subject of a chapter, although the second is divided into Chapters 2 and 3, respectively.

A practical spirituality like I propose is both helpful and illuminating, helpful because it attempts to re-claim the spiritual tradition of our Christian and Western heritage for the people today in much the same way as the Protestant Reformation reclaimed the scriptures for everyone: it made them accessible to all. The love and intention of God is truly for all persons and thus I am compelled to claim that that for which the monastics strive is available to all of us, regardless of one's abode or vocation. Simply put, perfection or deification, to use the vocabulary of the early church, is a possibility open to all people.

Such a practical spirituality is illuminating in that it re-interprets and clarifies issues previously perceived by the common person as strange and somehow beyond or above him or her in light of his or her daily experience and lack of formal theological training. My hope is to re-awaken the general believer (and non-believer) to the various pathways such issues illumine.

AMBIGUITY AND SIGNIFICANCE OF WORK

> Magical power,
>> marvelous action!
> Chopping wood,
>> carrying water...[1]

This ancient Chinese poem contains within its few lines the substance of my argument. Grappling with the nature of work is a task filled with ambiguity. At first, work seems a fairly straightforward activity to describe. One look in the dictionary, however, immediately dispels any such notion. *The American Heritage Dictionary* lists over 45 usages of the word. Work is an activity as well as an object. Work is both simple and complex.

How then to define work? Painters and professional basketball players, lawyers and musicians, assembly-line workers, teachers, and farmers differ both in their experience of work and also in how they distinguish work from and relate work to the other activities of their lives. Although the dictionary abounds with definitions it is helpful in distinguishing certain common senses of work.

We see that work is "physical or mental effort or activity directed toward the production or accomplishment of something; ...something that one is doing, making, or performing, especially as a part of one's occupation; a duty or task";[2] or "something made or done; result of effort: a work of art...."[3]

The sense of purpose necessary to and inherent in work should be highlighted. The dimension of purpose and meaning is common, and central, to any theology or spirituality of work.

...work ought to be an activity which helps a person to express their own personality and dreams.

Budden[4]

Each person has a unique talent and gift, and it is incumbent upon them to use it. Each of us must search for this special gift and then allow it to manifest through our life. Otherwise,it will be lost forever, and God's creation will be incomplete.

Martha Graham[5]

...human work is the intentional focusing of sufficiently disciplined energy upon the dream, or the design ...to effect its realization in some tangible medium. If work is withheld, the dream or intent is incapable of going further.

Douglas Steere[6]

Labor is the great reality in human life. In labor there is a truth of redemption and a truth of the constructive power of man [and woman].

Berdyaev[7]

Laying stress on the importance of work has a greater effect than any other technique of living in the direction of binding the individual more closely to reality.

Freud[8]

There is nothing better for a person than that they should eat and drink, and that they should make their soul enjoy good in their labor.

Ecclesiastes, The Bible[9]

The significant question is: "How can the soul enjoy good in its labor when there is no soul in the places where labor is organized ...?"[10] As Camus has written, "Without work all life goes rotten. But when work is soulless life stifles and dies."

In attempting to define the nature of work we find an array of descriptions reflecting, simply, the complexity of the phenomenon. What we need is an inclusive while not totally relative definition of work, a definition which recognizes work's many-sided characteristics but which includes them all rather than isolating each from the other and stratifying the various types and qualities of work.

Although my objective is to be inclusive, I am inclined to focus on the existential features of everyday work. Social, economic, and political aspects of work are addressed, but only secondarily. This is not a psychology of work nor an industrial sociology. Nor is it confronting social reality in the sense of my going out and interviewing people, for instance.

Despite my disagreement with Simone Weil's insistence on pain as a mode of liberation, I do agree with her contention that the true revolution to release the worker from oppression is, as she puts it, "...one of mind, body and spirit rather than a corporate solidarity of one social class against another. Healing of the fragmented self will come with a radical shift in gaze and posture...."[11] I find myself more and more in agreement with the viewpoint that a "true" revolution, and not merely the transfer of political and/or economic power from one group to another, is a cultural revolution. That is to say, fundamental and radical change will occur, if at all, at the level of the roots of a culture, and of a person. Clare Fischer's comment on Weil's theology of work is instructive:

> ...the lever that will release the proletariat from the yoke of oppression is not revolution, Weil concludes, but a transformation of the worker and the workers' culture; such a change will penetrate deeply into the flesh and touch the soul turning the head upward toward transcendent reality.[12]

LABOR, WORK, AND ACTION

In her book *The Human Condition*, Hannah Arendt proposes nothing less than "...a reconsideration of the human condition from the vantage point of our newest experiences and our most recent fears."[13] Her proposal is, she states, "...very simple: it is nothing more than to think what we are doing....[And that,] What we are doing, is indeed the central theme of this book."[14] Reflecting thus, Arendt clarifies the distinction between work *(homo faber)* and labor *(animal laborans)* and provides, among other things, the classical Hellenistic understanding of action and contemplation.

Arendt's definitions of labor, work, and action are instructive.

> Labor is the activity which corresponds to the biological process of the human body, whose spontaneous growth, metabolism, and eventual decay are bound to the vital necessities produced and fed into the life process by labor. The human condition of labor is life itself.[15]

The Greek term Arendt uses for labor is *animal laborans*. It refers to those who labor out of life's necessities and "mixes with" the things of the earth consuming itself in the process.[16]

> Work is the activity which corresponds to the unnaturalness of human existence, which is not imbedded in, and whose mortality is not compensated by, the species' ever-recurring life cycle. Work provides an "artificial" world of things, distinctly different from all natural surroundings. Within its borders each individual life is housed, while this world itself is meant to outlast and transcend them all. The human condition of work is worldliness.[17]

Homofaber, the Greek term used for work, also refers to one who makes and literally "works upon" the already gathered materials of the earth (stone, wood, etc.) "...fabricating the sheer unending variety of things whose sum total constitutes the human artifice."[18]

> Action, the only activity that goes on directly between men [and women] without the intermediary of things or matter, corresponds to the human condition of plurality, to the fact that men [and women], not Man, live on the earth and inhabit the world. While all aspects of the human condition are somehow related to politics, this plurality is specifically the condition ...of all political life.[19]

"All three activities and their corresponding conditions," Arendt informs us,

> are intimately connected with the most general condition of human existence: birth and death, natality and mortality. Labor assures not only individual survival, but the life of the species. Work and its product, the human artifact, bestow a permanence and durability upon the futility of mortal life and the fleeting character of human time. Action, in so far as it engages in founding and preserving political bodies, creates the condition for remembrance, that is, for history.[20]

Hannah Arendt's brilliant account of the place and function of labor, work, and action within *The Human Condition* (i.e., community), presents a clearly defined choice *between* labor and work.[21] Arendt articulates the importance of distinguishing labor *(animal laborans)* from work *(homo faber)*. The labor process is endless, "...caught in the cyclical movement of the body's life process [it] has neither a beginning nor an end."[22] The very mark of work or "fabrication," however, is "...to have a definite beginning and a definite, predictable end....[and] this characteristic alone distinguishes [it] ...from all other human activities."[23]

Much of the concept of *animal laborans* seems positive: the losing of one's self in one's work and becoming one (in harmony) with nature, with the life process. I agree with Arendt that the spiritual practitioners of the world's religious traditions, i.e., the contemplatives and mystics, recognized this type of work (manual or other labor that leaves the mind free for contemplation) as the most conducive for spiritual pursuits.[24] Such work is conducive to spiritual pursuits because it allows a person to still her or his mind, i.e., to be in the present, attentive to the task at hand. It allows a person to be attentive to the presence of God. In certain instances a person has the experience of being one with his or her work. Times of loosing one's self in one's work can be (although they are not necessarily so) the stepping stones toward spiritual fulfillment.[25]

Arendt's argument presents a dilemma: how can labor, which is the incorporation of the laborer into and with the very life process itself, be that activity of humanity which is *non*-worldly, which leads the person(s) involved away from "worldliness," to use Arendt's term. Granted, the result of labor is consumed and thus absorbed into the cyclical process of life, the process of non-stability or non-permanence, but how is that non-worldly? How can the process of life negate the very world in which we live? To what extent is freedom dependent upon worldliness? Can laborers be free? Is it possible for labor(ers) to transcend necessity, i.e., to achieve freedom, and if so, does it (do they) by that transcendence become work(ers)? or action (actors)?

However much we can appreciate Arendt's distinction between labor and work, I tend to believe that there is no fundamental difference between the two, at least for people addressing the issue of their lives today. Arendt's distinctions and clarifications of the movement and transformation of these themes—labor, work, action, and contemplation—through Western history are illuminating. They can help us begin to acknowledge and hopefully move beyond some of our societal contradictions and crises. However, we may not agree with the Hellenistic world view. Ultimately, we may decide that Plato and Aristotle and their precursors were mistaken when it comes to an understanding of the human condition with regard to labor and work (to leave action and contemplation aside for the moment). Perhaps, as a Christian, for instance, I may not view labor and work in a negative light. Arendt's argument is brilliant, but as a working person I do not find that her argument makes any difference how I respond to my situation.

My argument parallels Arendt's—with her sense of tension, i.e., the contemplative verses the active life—but she embraces the Hellenistic perspective which contrasts the two, holding them eternally apart. Here I am arguing that the dichotomy Arendt purports is irrelevant to contemporary peoples' lives, but the exploration of this tension is important because it is relevant to a spirituality of work.

Before proceeding it is important that we briefly pursue the ramifications of freedom and action and their possible impact on the political and economic spheres relative to the dignity, responsibility, and participation of persons--individual and collective workers.

Action is the mode of bringing the elements of fulfillment and freedom into the daily lives of the majority of people today. In other words, it is in the realm of action that the common lot of women and men can secure their human dignity; and this in the midst of their daily lives which are lived in the realm of work, which is to say in the realm of economics.

What would seem to be needed is to design a public arena in the world of economics. In other words, we need to re-interpret, to transform, the classical Greek perspective of the economy, defined as the private realm, in such a way that it incorporates the public realm into its very practice. In that transformation workers will inherit the possibility for action.

Yet the question can still be raised: "Is this not merely the emancipation of labor(ers) which Arendt clearly shows occurred at least a couple of centuries ago?"

In reply I can only say that I recognize Arendt's critique of the advent of a "social economy" and I do not mean to fall into that, unless by that term she would also preclude the possibility of "politicizing" the economy; for that is precisely what I am proposing (if I understand Arendt correctly, re: "politics"). That is, I am suggesting that by incorporating, in the very places where they work, means by which workers can act—by speech and by deed—we would, thereby, be building politics into the very structure of the economy.

Another question presents itself: "Do you mean to say that we could thereby overcome the dilemma of merely making public private activity, to paraphrase Arendt, which Arendt says is all that is possible in a social economy?"

To this I respond, if politics is that public arena in which a person can act through speech and/or deed, and thereby transcend necessity through the practice of freedom, then the structuring into the economy, i.e., the workplace, of this possibility for action would overcome the Hellenic dichotomy which forever delegates the economical and the political into separate camps.

Specifically, I am thinking of the many variants of "workplace democracy" and "economic democracy," in which workers participate in the decision-making apparatus of their workplace. However, as with political democracy, there is the need for the "citizens" (workers) to "own" the body politic (the particular economic body, in this case) which is to say, there is the necessity of *control*.

It is my contention that laborers/workers can transcend their mode of being (laboring), arrested as they are by necessity, and enter the realm of action and freedom by the incorporation of a specifically political dimension into their place of labor.

"But will it not still be labor?"

Yes, I think it will. But the people themselves will no longer be strictly laborers. And this gets back to the issue regarding the inapplicableness of Arendt's distinction for working and laboring people themselves. I do not think she would agree that one can be "employeed" in labor and *at the same time* be a truly political actor, which in her understanding is to be truly human. Whereas, I do think it is possible. Indeed, I think it is the only way out of the modern dilemma in which society is held captive.

An important distinction to make between the classical Greeks and contemporary society is that today the economy is vastly more comprehensive, involving much more that simply the "home." Economic structures and bodies are central to our society and they influence, indeed, they direct much of our political agenda.

Where Arendt stands on this issue I am not sure, but it seems to me that there is a "necessity" of inoculating the economic arena with politics; specifically and forthrightly. If this is a capitulation to the denigrating process of the victory of *animal laborans*, so be it. Are we, rather, to impose a benevolent dictatorship of a new feudal order in which the "free men" with the time and the means for "political" activity can tend the flock of the masses? If not, the alternative is to dismantle the factories and other places of work, and to eliminate or forswear all the new technologies, which by their very nature require the de-humanization of the people laboring to produce and maintain them. Close the factories, the very system of which denies the possibility of action and speech, of freedom (and thereby responsibility) and politics. Otherwise, politicize them.

Why? In order to liberate the people in them not so much from the "curse" of labor but from the denial of their human dignity, and for the possibility of being free (Arendt's term for political beings) men and women.

THE DIALECTICAL NATURE OF WORK

Articulating the difference between work and labor is important as we analyze our world and the human enterprise. As I reflect on work as it relates to spirituality, it is apparent to me that the various distinctions are actually dialectical or dialogical, describing the two sides of the *same* coin, not two different coins. In this case the coin is human effort. Consequently, from this point on I use the term "work" inclusively.

Our dilemma is that we have attempted to dichotomize a dialectical phenomenon. Work includes both the process and the goal, it is both painful effort and the means of overcoming obstacles. Jesuit theologian Jean Lacroix expresses the dialectical nature of work well when he writes, "work is a sign of alienation. But it is a remedy also to this alienation....[It is] at the same time passiveness and activeness, adjustment to the object and submission to the subject, insertion of [humanity] in the world and transfiguration of that world."[26]

Work for Lacroix is dynamic, its "...privileged role...comes...from the fact that it is a *mediator between nature and freedom*: its perpetual danger is to bog [humanity] down in nature and to naturalize [humanity], its greatness is to be for humanity the most efficacious factor of liberation."[27] The dynamic quality of work is transforming, especially in light of the "...bond between achievement and joy [which] is characteristic of human work...."[28] Lacroix continues, echoing the scholastic philosophers, "to work is to make oneself while producing an achievement, to perfect oneself while perfecting the world. Consequently the aim of work is dual, ...perfection of the work and perfection of the worker."[29]

Lacroix, like Arendt, makes helpful distinctions between work and, in this case, contemplation. Between them I favor Lacroix, but I disagree with him regarding the vast separation he posits between the two modes. I think it possible to participate in both contemplation and work at the same time. In other words, I think one can practice contemplation while at work.

The French Jesuit, Joseph Thomas, illuminates the dialetical nature of work in light of three Biblical perspectives: the penitential, the creationist, and the eschatological. Each approach illustrates one aspect of work, all are necessary for a comprehensive picture. In the penitential perspective, humanity is condemned to work; as expressed in Genesis, "You will earn your bread by the sweat of your brow." The creationist relies on a different passage from Genesis: "dominate the earth and bring it under submission." Humanity is seen according to this approach as the image of God because we are creators, too. Whereas the first is a pessimistic view, this second view is decidedly optimistic. "The first creation is continued; the creative action of God constantly renews itself through the action of the [person] at work. Every creative effort becomes the meeting point where [people] come into union with God."[30]

Because my sympathy lies with the creationist perspective, it is important to include the following statement concerning its inherent drawbacks.

> First of all, it has little to say to those for whom work offers no element of creativity but only monotony and virtual enslavement. Second, the creationist's enthusiasm for innovation and progress cannot justify of itself the effort it entails. Without a clear goal or end for human work, any action of man [or woman] would be justified in the long run, provided it were new and done with ardor. Such a viewpoint could open the way to new forms of paganism, idolatry, and slavery.[31]

Lacking a "clear goal or end," Thomas adds the third approach amplifying the second. The eschatological view of work considers work's "...function in the progress of humanity toward the kingdom to come."[32] This perspective instills work with promise and vision, it places work within the context of hope. Furthermore, "...the eschatological view has the merit of indicating a path to synthesis,"[33] because it supplies a unifying center ("the triumphant Christ"[34]) lacking in the first and second approaches.

Louis Savary in *Man: His World and His Work* (1967), concludes his review of Thomas' three views of work with a series of questions concerning the significance of the "final Christ" for work and the world, and questions about the relationship of work to the kingdom of God. In response to Savary's questions, it appears that the transformative dynamic which I propose is the element that ties together the various strands of Savary's questions. For instance, the "religious 'consistency' of work and of each one's pain" could be that dynamic of transformation, that process of inner effort, of working on one's self. Again, that which "the final Christ" shares "with the present becoming of the world and with the labor of each [person]" is, also, the dynamic of transformation—the dynamic of becoming, of processing toward being. As each person labors—intentionally—in the world, so they are aligning themselves with Christ, and thus transforming themselves, and the world, through their work.

Pope John Paul II provides another and more recent "theology of work" in his encyclical letter of September, 1981, *Laborem Exercens*. Central to John Paul II's argument is his insistence upon Humanity[35] "...as the Subject of Work." The sources of the dignity of work are to be sought in the worker (in the subject) and not in the kind of work (the objective dimension). "Work is for [humanity] not [humanity] for work."[36]

Among his "Elements for a Spirituality of Work" (Section V), particularly striking is the one regarding the necessity of "an inner effort,"[37] that an inner effort is needed in order that work may be salvific. That is to say, merely because a person works does not necessarily imply that he or she is being sanctified in and through the work itself.

It is not the *kind* of work that bestows value but, rather, the worker him or herself *is* the value—and the work is a *means* to help realize the potential of that value. However, to fully realize one's potential each person must exert an effort, an inner effort, to align him or herself with the divine will. Each person must, if he or she is to sanctify his or her work, and through that his own or her own self, be purposeful in his or her work/life. That is to say, the person sanctifies the work, *his or her* work, through the effort they bring to it; the type or kind of work is not the determining factor in this sanctification. Each person has the choice to cooperate, or not, with the work of creation. By its very nature this work, this co-creation, this sacramentalizing of all of life, involves both an inner and an outer dimension.

The inner dimension is this "inner effort" on the part of each person in the midst of their everyday work/life. Likewise, their efforts are extended to the outer activities at and by which they occupy their day(s). John Paul II is equally clear that the work people do in the world becomes the continuing creation of the world. It becomes God's work, for by that work humanity grows in knowledge and also in community. We humans are co-creators with God and it is in and with our outer work, illuminated as it is by our inner work, that the human community builds itself and participates in the divine plan.

An important question to ask as we explore the nature of the tensions inherent in work and spirituality is, "What link is there between the work of humanity and the kingdom of God?" This is the same query D.M. Dooling et al. raise in relationship to craftsmanship: "Is there something special about the person-at-work that serves the

universe in a special way, something related to the way we're created?"[38]

TENSIONS

> From the same word which is the root of "art" and
> "order" comes the carpenter's word for "joinery" in
> Greek, *harmos*, from which comes "harmony."[39]

As I have attempted to show in discussing the different understandings of the nature of work and especially of the distinction
between labor and work, there is a tension not only between the
different terms and concepts but also between the proponents of the
various definitions and understandings. There *is* a tension between
labor and work, between theology and ethics and spirituality, between
action and contemplation. The tension, however, is not ultimate, it is
not final. The above quote illustrates my contention that it is *within*
our work that we may seek to "join" the various poles of our lives. The
"special-ness" about the person-at-work is the real possibility of using
this tension to fabricate a harmony: a harmony of our lives and of our
being.

Humanity is the link between God and animal, the bridge between heaven and earth. The means by which we can bring heaven
down to earth is through humans, through human activity. Through a
practical spirituality of work, i.e., in and through work, humans can be
"...the receiver(s) and transmitter(s) of forces of creation much greater than [themselves]."[40] In keeping with this theme of linking different
levels is the following understanding of work: "...a way in which
[people] may create and cross a bridge in [themselves] and center
[themselves] in [their] own essential unity."[41] As such, I propose in my
spirituality of work ways to heal the tensions we experience in our
lives so that we may experience our essential unity. In the following
paragraphs I clarify these tensions: contemplation and work; inner
and outer; worship and work; sacred verses secular and spirit verses
matter. The graph on the following page is an attempt to visually
piece together the various elements of a spiritual theology of work. It
needs to be a three-dimensional graph to truly represent the inter-
relatedness of the parts.

YWHW/GOD

Jesus Christ

Holy Spirit

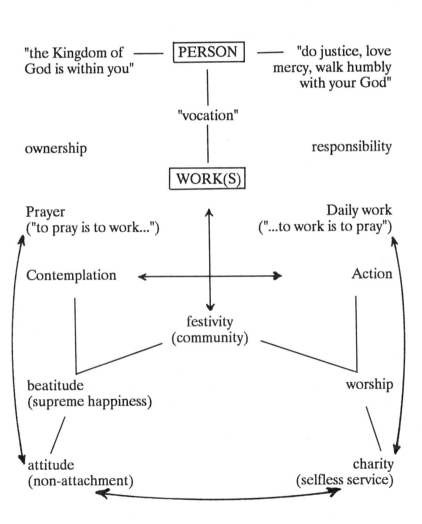

"the Kingdom of ——— [PERSON] ——— "do justice, love
God is within you"   mercy, walk humbly
                                                          with your God"

"vocation"

ownership   responsibility

[WORK(S)]

Prayer   Daily work
("to pray is to work...")   ("...to work is to pray")

Contemplation ←——————————→ Action

festivity
(community)

beatitude   worship
(supreme happiness)

attitude   charity
(non-attachment)   (selfless service)

Contemplation and Work

Foremost among the tensions we experience is the split between contemplation and work. From the time of the Hellenists we have heard that the active life and the contemplative life are mutually exclusive. The interests and demands of the one are diametrically opposed to the other, so the argument runs. This tension will be dealt with in depth in chapter two. At the moment it is important to state that I am not denying the tension. What I am saying is that the tension can be overcome. Indeed, I see the tension as simply the two sides of the same coin. Both "sides," therefore, are real and active ingredients of the total picture. Difficulties arise when we view the two sides as distinct realities, as separate entities, rather than as contrasting or complimentary parts of a whole.

Inner Work and Outer Work

Often separated, the inner and the outer lives of persons are in actuality parts of a greater whole. Their separation results in a schizo-phrenic existence for individuals as well as for societies. If we would live with integrity, integrally, we must forge a union between and betwixt our inner and outer lives; between contemplation and work. The intimate bond between contemplation and work understood in light of our inner and outer lives is well expressed by Douglas Steere as he paraphrases Immanuel Kant: "...one might say of work and contemplation that work without contemplation is bitter and blind, but that contemplation without work is callow and empty."[42] In forging such a union we must acknowledge the tension inherent in the relationship of the inner and the outer but, in the process, we must realize that both our inner work and our outer work can and need to be aimed toward the same goal—our spiritual fulfillment.

Pope John Paul II illuminates the importance of inner work as it relates to outer work in the final section of *Laborem Exercens*, "Elements for a Spirituality of Work."

> An inner effort on the part of the human spirit, guided
> by faith, hope, and charity, is needed in order that
> ...the work of the individual human being may be

given the meaning which it has in the eyes of God and
by means of which work enters into the salvation
process on a par with the other ordinary yet particularly important components of its texture.[43]

The key to holding contemplation and work together is the disposition conveyed by the Desert Fathers and throughout *The Philokalia*:
be at work with your hands but have your mind/heart with God. It is
possible to engage in both contemplation and work at the same time.
These issues are discussed in more detail in Chapter 2.

Worship and Work

The pervasive connection is art, which can help to heal the split
between worship and work. Other agents for healing are persons' attitudes, and charity or selfless service. I am, however, undecided as to
the resolution of this tension. I see that both worship and work are
necessary. I see that there is an alternating rhythm between them—
and this I accept as good, even necessary—but I want to differentiate
between worship and rest. One can be worshipful while working;
worship does not always imply rest or repose. It is not necessary for a
person to be at rest for her or him to worship. Worship can be, and
should be, a countenance held by a person. A person may be worship-
ing—and thereby also, serving—God while working. And thus, the
workplace can be a worship(ful) place, regardless of the amount or
intensity of activity.

Yet, the sense of balance, of rhythm, is important. And here I
want to be sure to include *festivity*, the need of the festive in human
life, in order to be whole and complete. This is elaborated upon in
Chapter 3.

Sacred vs. Secular and Spirit vs. Matter

There is a need to transcend the false duality posed between the
sacred and the so-called secular in the social realm, and between spirit
and matter in the personal realm. I address these issues in both Chapter 2 (from a more philosophical and theological level, as pertaining

to spirituality itself) and Chapter 4 (from a socio-ethico perspective).

I do not deny that there is a tension but, rather, that the sense of dualism, of two opposing and conflicting realms, is false. There is no fence, no dividing line between spirit and matter. Physicists discovered many years ago that matter is nothing but contracted, concentrated energy; that the small units composing the atom have the properties of both particles *and* waves. Our brains are directly affected by the food we eat and the air we breath. There is no dividing line between the inner and the outer. At one moment the air we breath is "outside" and a moment later it is "inside." Verily, as the Hindu tradition states "Thou art That." The world is of a piece, it is whole, it is ONE. Unity, and not duality, is the reality. All of life is sacred. To cite another tradition, contemporary Eastern Orthodox Christians declare that, "In the context of the Church's liturgical understanding of humanity, world, society and history, any division between the verticalism [the sacred/divine] and horizontalism [the worldly] is not merely absurd but actually heretical!"[44]

Douglas Steere, a North American Quaker and philosophy professor, proposes in his book *Work and Contemplation*, a means to transcend this false duality. Steere writes about the "sacrament of the present moment"[45] in which a person attends to each and every task, encounter, and moment of his or her life as a sacrament, as being in the presence of God. A section of Chapter 4 is addressed to this. Two other empowering factors discussed in Chapter 4 are those of the intrinsic worth of each person and each occupation, and the role of work in building community.

Another way of overcoming the tension we experience between spirit and matter is articulated by D.M. Dooling and other north American writers in the book quoted above, *A Way of Working*. Using the experience of the artisan and the imagery of alchemy these writers weave a splendid and illuminating pageant of human drama, struggle, and fulfillment.

Saint Maximus the Confessor, a seventh-century Greek theologian, exemplifies the Eastern Orthodox Christian perspective of a unitary creation. Maximus speaks eloquently of Humanity as "a living workshop"[46] in which spirit and matter are formed consubstantially into a new union and being: true(ly) Humanity. Here, in Maximus, are ideas and images which bring together so many of the different strands I have been working with: unity, deification, alchemy, work, humanity as co-creator. Though I have not done a detailed study of Maximus' writings, nor have I used him extensively in this book, Maximus has provided a central guiding image—humanity as a living workshop—and a fundamental source within the Christian tradition of the Unity of creation.

2

SPIRITUALITY

In this chapter I reflect on some necessary ingredients for a who-listic spirituality: spirituality both practical and worldly, and accessible to men and women in all walks of life; a spirituality both inclusive and complete: inclusive in that all of life is encompassed, including the variety of religious traditions in human experience; complete in that opposites and tensions and disparate elements and entities are seen to be in relationship to one another in the same way as the two sides of a coin are joined together in one unit(y). I attempt to articulate this dynamic relationship by way of three illustrative but also essential tensions: that between (1) inner and outer, (2) prayer and work, and (3) contemplation and action. I rely largely on my study of work in the Christian monastic tradition.

Understanding spirituality requires more than a reading of the latest "pop" magazine article. We must undertake a study of the world's religious, philosophical, literary, historical, and artistic tradi-tions if we would claim even amateur status in the field. I am not writing a "Christian" spirituality of work. Though I focus on Christian experience, and though most of my argument centers around Chris-tian themes and writers, my intention is to provide a contemporary, inclusive, and practical understanding and approach to work and spir-ituality. Therefore, wisdom and insight are gleaned from a compara-tive study. While as individuals we may, and indeed probably must, choose our path, our "one" way, such a choice by no means eliminates nor de-legitimizes truths found on other paths manifested in other religions and traditions. In addition to and, in truth, more important than the standard scholarly disciplines, a study of spirituality demands practical, first-hand engagement. Without a sustained, personal expe-rience the realms of the spirit will remain foreign territory. The scrip-tural adage, "knock and it shall be opened, seek and you shall find," is both appropriate and necessary for entry to the spiritual: it is some-thing not found in books, although books may help expand one's awareness or wet one's appetite.

What, then, is spirituality? How do we begin? How do we discover what "real," wholistic spirituality is?

Spirituality is that attraction and movement of the human soul (person) toward God or the divine. Spirituality is what humans do in response to God's call. Spirituality is that which leads a person closer to God, to union and thus wholeness. Spirituality, for my purposes, encompasses three general areas of focus: (1) inner work and outer work; (2) contemplation and action; and (3) prayer and work. Each area involves a dynamic tension or dialectic and not a dichotomy or exclusiveness. Each area is part of the whole; no one area is complete unto itself. A wholistic (or holistic) spirituality must, of necessity, include all three.

To be whole, holy, and inclusive, spirituality must encompass and incorporate both poles in all three areas. It will not do to have a spirituality of only prayer and contemplation, for a person lives in the world and by the very fact of breathing is inextricably bound to both the inner and the outer realms of creation.

Wholistic spirituality must be applicable for all people in all circumstances; it must incorporate all of a person's life rather than being only one more part or appendage to an already full and compartmentalized, and perhaps cluttered, existence. A spirituality that is whole incorporates all aspects of our being—body, mind, feelings, spirit—as well as of our daily existence—work, play, relationships, career, religion, politics, etc. Ordinary women and men who must work for a living (i.e., either do not have the calling for a monastic vocation or do not have the leisure resulting from being independently wealthy) can pursue spiritual fulfillment in their everyday lives. Wholistic spirituality means just that, "whole." It means the whole thing: all of life and creation. As such, it includes both the sense of inclusiveness (every one or thing: all) as well as the sense of completeness (a unit/y).

All of life is subject matter (the working field) for spirituality: for knowing the divine. Prayer is work, or at least it has been for many of the great contemplatives and mystics of the Christian tradition. In truth, throughout the patristic era and even up to the present time (at least in the Christian East), monastics and others have talked about the life of prayer as the "active life." The call for a wholistic spirituality is a call for life to be whole. It is a call for life to be more than a potpourri of separate, isolated bits and pieces. It is a call for life to be complete and integrated. We can and must learn to know God in our work as well as in our prayer.

The unnamed pilgrim in the spiritual classic, *The Way of a Pilgrim*, asks, upon hearing St. Paul's admonition to "pray unceasingly" (1 Thessolonians 5:17), "How?!" That is *the* question, and I believe it is a question being asked today by many people, Christians and non-Christians alike.

THE SIGNIFICANCE OF
WHOLISM AND UNITY

At this point, I will address the significance of wholism and the weakness of dualism as world views and foundations for philosophy or theology—and for a spirituality of work.

My position is that of radical wholism. I am convinced of the ONE-ness of God and of creation, and find any position based on a dualistic outlook to be both detrimental to personal and social well-being and also, heretical to the Christian faith. I see life composed not of dichotomies, where never the twain shall meet, but, rather, of dialectical relationships. Life is a situation of both-and rather than of either-or.

First, I would like to highlight one of the more intriguing articulations of the Orthodox Christian theological tradition, which for Orthodox includes the spiritual. This position that humans are "living workshops," and all of creation is a unity, is of primary importance for it illuminates the entire field of practical spirituality.

Saint Maximus the Confessor (668 AD) represents a line of thought developed by the Cappadocian Fathers: Basil the Great (330–379), Gregory of Nazianzus (329–389), and especially Gregory of Nyssa (c.330–c.395).[1] Maximus speaks of each person as a *living* "*workshop.*" A person, through the grace of God in Jesus Christ and the active work of the Holy Spirit, undergoes a transformation in which he or she is "divinized" or brought to perfection ("deification," *theopisis*). Maximus speaks of the consubstantiality of matter and spirit. It is the dynamic tension between matter and spirit, both of which are inherent and essential to truly human existence, which generates and realizes this transformation. It is a process of bringing matter into tune or harmony with spirit but, contrary to dualism, it does not result in the elimination or denigration of matter. Rather, matter is transformed to its proper state, that is, divination or union with God.

According to the school to which Maximus belonged, "Man" (the nature of Man [sic] and not individuals) is defined as a "microcosm." As articulated by the late French theologian M.D. Chenu:

> Man [sic] epitomizes in [it]self the elements and the values of the cosmos, statically, at the highest point of creation, and dynamically, owing to [its] physical and moral duality in a hierarchic ascent towards the supreme Unity. If this physical system is seen as the realization of God's design, it takes on a religious meaning which does not conflict with the internal laws of each of the natures, these laws are the expression of the divine plan.[2]

Maximus bases his theology on unity. God is the Supreme Unity, God is one; and God is the unifying force in all things which holds all things together. This operation of unification is, as Maximus terms it, a "synthesis" of which the individual parts are maintained and the essences of each respected. The synthesis or unification is accomplished by the dynamic process in the world as it moves toward unity.[3]

Humanity ("Man") is a unity of body and soul. As a microcosm, cosmic nature is innate in humanity, and thus, the unification of the cosmos is accomplished by and in humanity. Indeed, humanity plays a central, crucial role in the cosmic scheme of unification as we imitate God the Creator. For, "humanity by its nature is the *fabricator* of the universe, reunifying it in a new ascent towards that unity from which it was created."[4]

Explaining the implication of Maximus' term "fabricator," Chenu says the essential word for interpreting this text is the Greek word *ergasterion*, derived from *ergon* meaning "work." This word is of great importance because

> ...it describes the action by which [humanity] confronts, takes hold of, transforms and conquers nature, "realizing" it by a unification which to the Greeks was

the final perfecting of an object. (The content of the
Latin *labor*, which is part of the concept of "work," is
consequently quite irrelevant.) The Latin translation,
somewhat clumsy but equally significant, is *officina*. In
French it is *atelier* or *usine*; in English "workshop" or
"factory." Here the word loses something of its sense
of personal action, the action of a "workman" in his [or
her] work, as it were biologically.[5]

This commentary also illustrates the earlier distinction between the
concepts originally conveyed with the words "work" and "labor" in
chapter one.

Again, in Maximus' words:

Man [sic] is a living workshop which functions
permanently and continuously. [Humanity it] self is
the unifying element of the most widely differing realities, in all their diversity, for good and in beauty,
according to the origin of each entity. [Humanity it]
self is divided into male and female, but possesses, by
[its] nature, a capacity for total synthesis.

This unifying power, working in the causal evolution of these various entities, thus reveals the great
mystery of the divine plan, since it harmonizes the
mutual cohesion of opposites, from the nearest to the
farthest, from the smallest to the greatest, and so leads
them back progressively to their unity in God.

In this design [humanity], last of created beings, is
a factor of physical unity, accomplishing a universal
synthesis between all extremes by their own components. In so doing [it] returns them all to God as their
first cause, assembling them primarily in a unity based
on their autonomy and on their previous disparity,
then leading them, in ordered progress, in an exalting
and unifying ascent, which will end all differences, to
God.[6]

Underlying this view of humanity's role and relationship with nature is the concept of the consubstantial union of matter and spirit. In effect, this concept holds that "any separation between the body and the soul of humanity destroys or unbalances, to the extent of the separation..., this fundamental relationship between humanity and nature, which the Greeks called *techne*, because it imperils the very nature of the 'microcosm'."[7]

Once again the connectedness of body and soul is apparent. We see that the inner and the outer are intimately intertwined in such a fashion that there can be no realistic distinction between one and the other; what occurs in one simultaneously affects, and thus occurs in, the other. The boundary between the inner and the outer is, literally, only a breath of air.

Also, from this brief review of Maximus' theology, we glimpse the connection and importance of "work" in the human agenda. As the "fabricator" of the universe, humanity's activities, or work, are part and parcel of salvation (history, evolution). Work is an intrinsic function of the incarnate spirit. We see that all of creation is the proper realm of humanity's activity and self-fulfillment.

WEAKNESS OF DUALISM

Based on any dualistic scheme, spirituality becomes that part of life in which persons seek to align themselves, by one means or another, with the forces of good over-against evil. The key word in the previous sentence is "part." Life understood in view of dualism is composed of *parts*. These various parts are sometimes in cooperation but more likely in competition or outright conflict. Thus, "spiritual life" is that part of life in which a person is aligning herself or himself with the good, with the spirit. And it is over-against her or his "earthly" life of "matter" and "flesh."

What has been problematic throughout human history is the struggle to live well on this earth *and* in this body (with its variety of appetites and desires), while, at the same time, trying to find a way out—out of this earth, out of this body, out of this predicament. How do we reconcile seemingly contrasting qualities? How do we live productively? How do we live abundantly? How, indeed, if we are told to deny ourselves; if we are told to deny this body we inhabit? There is a problem, and it would seem to be attached to the human condition.

Humanity is, however, too multi-hued and diverse to be locked into only one or two cultures holding to a dualistic world view. The Hebrews, for example, were not dualistic, and Christianity, obviously, shares a common heritage. Biblical thought claims the person is a person because he or she is incarnated: because he or she has a body. We are incarnated spirit and what makes us what we are is the *combination* of spirit and body.

Native Americans are not dualistic. Neither are the indigenous peoples of Siberia, the Pacific Islands, nor China, to name a few. Though there is dualism within the parthenon of South Asian thought and religion, many of the profound thinkers and religious traditions of India are decidedly monistic (and most definitely wholistic). Kashmir Shaivism, for example, espouses a profound unity of life.

The Bible does not separate the horizontal and the vertical dimensions, either

> ...in terms of a dualism between religion and politics, between the love of God and love for one's neighbor, between religious conduct and human conduct. On the contrary, the tendency of Jesus is firmly to hold on to the unity of these two lines of conduct. ...life does not consist in two parallel paths, but essentially in their meeting and in their intersection.[8]

Jesus and the writers of the Bible practice a consciousness of unity, and to accept such a distinction—horizontal vs. vertical—is "the most subtle form of atheism."[9] Jesus believes in one world which belongs entirely to the Kingdom of God. In his teaching there is no dualism, no "separation of the different domains of existence."[10]

INNER AND OUTER

All traditional ways of life (cultural as well as strictly "religious") recognize both an inner and an outer work in the human drama. To the best of my knowledge, all of them place a priority on the inner work, the outer being a means toward the end of which the inner is the essence.[11] Orthodox Christianity expresses the relationship of the inner and the outer in the following manner.

> ...as St. Nikodimos puts it in his introduction...the
> texts of *The Philokalia* are... "a mystical school of
> inward prayer" where those who study may cultivate
> the divine seed implanted in their hearts at baptism
> and so grow in spirit that they become "sons of God,"
> attaining through deification "the measure of the stat-
> ure of the fulness [sic] of Christ." The emphasis is
> therefore on inner work, on the cleansing of "the in-
> side of the cup and plate, so that their outside may
> also be clean." This does not mean that what one
> might call outer work—the keeping of the command-
> ments and the practice of the moral virtues—is of no
> importance. On the contrary, such work is a precondi-
> tion of that purification without which no real prog-
> ress in inner work can be made. Indeed, in this respect
> outer and inner complement one another. Atrophy or
> defeat follow only when outer work is practiced as an
> end in itself, and the one thing needful—the inner
> practice of guarding the intellect and of pure
> prayer—is neglected.[12]

If we, as humans, as persons, are whole at least in potential, we
are, then, one and not dual. As such, there is no difference between
the inner and the outer. We do not have one life we live "inside" our
skin or our brain, inside our heart and mind, and another life which
we live "outside" breathing the air, walking the streets, reading books,
playing ball, or working on the farm or in the office. The proof lies
with the example used: the air "outside" which we breath becomes by
the very act itself air "inside" by which our bodies (including brain and
heart) collect oxygen in order to survive. When we read the information of this page the information is processed *into* us, via our eyes,
brain, and nervous system, only to return "outside" again via mouths if
speaking or hands if writing, making, or doing. As one wise sage put
the question: "Where is God not?"

There is no difference between the inner and the outer. We are of
a oneness. This oneness may be split asunder; it may be forgotten or
denied; but it is still the nature of human existence.

It is often argued that we do not experience a oneness. This may be true, but that does not disprove that fundamentally we are created whole. An individual may say, however, or point to the fact that we must work on ourselves in order to realize or recognize our innate oneness. Perhaps the Christian terminology of "original sin" gets at this split in our lived situation: a split which needs to be healed if we are to be integrated persons, if we are to be faithful to God's design.

The work on ourselves which accompanies our daily work is the means of mending our alienation from nature as well as mending our separation from each other and from ourselves. But, of course, our daily work, what we do with our lives from day to day and during each day, is the field in which the means are actualized and made manifest. It is not enough to say that the only way to perfection is the quiet of a monastery. Jesus and his disciples, to use them as examples, never lived in monasteries. Surely they spent some time in quiet, in contemplation and prayer, but their lives were lived among people in the daily concourse of commerce and agriculture. The monastery has always been for the few (and there is no problem with that); it has not been the way of life for the vast majority of people. It is a full-time occupation for only some, but it provides others the opportunity for rest and contemplation. In this way it is part of the rhythm of life and can be a very natural component of a person's life of balance.

Since the majority of us do not, and will not, live monastic lives it becomes essential that we develop ways to find our spiritual fulfillment in everyday living. All of life is sacred. All of life is under God's purvey. It is wrong understanding to say "I worship God at church, but at home or at work anything goes." There is no place where God is not present. There is no time when we are not present to the reality of our selves and our lives.

We humans are the fulcrum of time and space; of history and meaning. All the forces of good and evil, of beauty and ugliness, of life and death, past and present, collide in each individual person. To deny we are in the presence of God at all times is absurd. Where are the walls? Where are the fences between now and then; between home and work and worship? Does the air not enter all of life? Does not thought and feeling go where ever we go? Where is God not present? When are we not with ourselves?

It is in and with our everyday lives that we are going to find our spiritual fulfillment. It is only here—which is everywhere and everything—that we will realize our being and purpose.

Striving for such fulfillment calls forth each person's every trait and characteristic in his or her endeavor to forge a life of integrity and meaning. In forging a harmony between the inner and the outer we discover the necessity of acting, of reflecting on our action, and of seeking the source of "true" or "right" action.

CONTEMPLATION AND ACTION

> The world is full of ideas, said the Ancients. Work, which gives ideas birth, is a major act of adult men [and women] and should not be considered,...as opposed to contemplation. The Christian [person] of wisdom...finds unity in the combination of these two functions.[13]

> He [or she] who neglects action and depends on theoretical knowledge holds a staff of reed instead of a double-edged sword....[14]

> Even though knowledge is true, it is still not firmly established if unaccompanied by works. For everything is established by being put into practice.[15]

> It remains a paradox of the mystics that the passivity at which they appear to aim is really a state of the most intense activity: more, that where it is wholly absent no great creative action can take place.[16]

Thus we enter the elusive realm of contemplation, at the heart of any spirituality, *and* of action.

Arendt, as we saw in Chapter 1, argues the case for a strong distinction between work and labor and between the active and the contemplative life. It seems more accurate from the perspective of practical spirituality, however, that Arendt's differences are not real. The truth of the matter is that there is no dichotomy but, rather, a oneness or, for that matter, even a dialectic. What may appear as disparate parts are merely the lost or misplaced members of the one body.

At this point I will review the understandings held by those of the spiritual path called mystics. Mysticism is not some other-worldly escape from the "realities" of life but rather, as Evelyn Underhill puts it, "True mysticism is active and practical, not passive and theoretical. It is an organic life-process, a something which the whole self does; not something as to which its intellect holds an opinion."[17] For mystics contemplation is the active life. What remains for me to show and for us today to realize—and subsequently make manifest—is that the active life may also be contemplative.

The Russian theologian and staretz[18] Theophan the Recluse (1815–94) states:

> There are two ways to become one with God: the active way and the contemplative way. The first is for Christians who live in the world, the second for those who have abandoned all worldly things. But in practice neither way can exist in total isolation from the other. Those who live in the world must also keep to the contemplative way in some measure. As I told you before, you should accustom yourself to remember the Lord always and to walk always before His face. That is what is meant by the contemplative way.... The body at work but the thought with God—such should be the state of a true Christian.... [T]his must be your guiding principle: work with your hands and yet remain with God in mind and heart.[19]

While living the contemplative life in the world we must remember to exhale as well as to inhale. Though we breathe in the thoughts and contemplate our situation, we must not forget to breathe out by working in the world.[20]

Douglas Steere has stated this integral connection of contemplation and action and everyday work in these words: "If contemplation is required to give a frame of meaning and significance to work; work, and curiously enough, manual work, in which the body and its co-ordination are in some way involved, has a contribution to make to the ordering of the very psyche that does the contemplating."[21]

The early Christians, the "Fathers," et al., "had no intention of making the active and the contemplative into two separate vocations or two distinct forms of...life which would be pursued by different individuals. They are two aspects of the one Christian life which exists side by side in the vocation of every Christian."[22] If there is now a split between the two forms of life it is an aberration of modernity; it underlies modern humanity's alienation.

> The loss of a vital contact with the Scriptures and the liturgy, which gradually came about in the late Middle Ages, was responsible for the breakdown of this unity (of the active and the contemplative). The Christian of the sixteenth century had little contact with the Word of God, because the Bible had become largely a closed book, and the liturgy, which had become fossilized, had ceased to perform its function of proclaiming the divine Word. Consequently the imagination was used to supply food for the soul which had previously been provided by these living sources. Meditation was then conceived of as an exercise of discursive reasoning operating upon some object of faith and designed to stir up images in the imagination which would give rise to affective acts. The effect of this development was to oppose medita- tion to contemplative prayer....[23]

Those sources quoted at the beginning of this section illuminate means by which harmony might be achieved. One is the blending of the active and the contemplative, the other is the alternating of the two.

An example of the second approach is the Benedictine daily schedule interspersing designated times for prayer and other times for work. Each person therefore has both active and contemplative time and endeavors, no one person limited to a single function. Benedict, however, did strive in his monasteries to combine action and contem- plation.

Saint Gregory the Great, as the author of *The Life of Benedict*, is a major force and source in the propagation of Benedictine thought and practice. Gregory first formulated the Benedictine idea of con-

templation,[24] which differed significantly from the Egyptian idea.
Cuthbert Butler shows in his important study, *Benedictine Monachism,* "...that for St. Gregory the two lives are not lived apart by two
sets of [people]. They are to be combined in the life of each one."[25]
Indeed, Gregory never entertained the conception of separating the
contemplative and the active, as did Cassian and the Egyptian her-
mits. Rather, St. Gregory's

> ...only conception of a contemplative life is one in
> which active good works hold a considerable, and
> even, in point of time, a predominant place; but in
> which for all that, the effort to exercise also the works
> of the contemplative life is kept habitually in opera-
> tion. It is, in short, a "mixed life," wherein each of the
> two lives is really and fully lived....And so a Benedic-
> tine monk, while he carries out his allotted works of
> the active life, must keep alive an unflagging love and
> desire of the contemplative life and its works, and
> must at steadily recurring intervals make the effort to
> give himself up to contemplation: and, so doing, he
> has St.Gregory's assurance that he holds on to the
> contemplative life in its entireness, without infidelity
> or instability.[26]

Gregory viewed the contemplative life neither as a special privi-
lege for those elect few of humankind somehow chosen to be saints
nor as a thing of supernatural qualities reserved for "holy" people. "On
the contrary, [Gregory] believed it to be within the reach of all
[people] of goodwill who give themselves seriously to prayer and keep
due guard on their hearts."[27] Gregory himself states:

> It is not the case that the grace of contemplation is
> given to the highest and not given to the lowest; but
> often the highest, and often the most lowly, and very
> often those who have renounced (*remoti*), and some-
> times also those who are married, receive it. If there-
> fore there is no state of life of the faithful from which
> the grace of contemplation can be excluded, any one
> who keeps his [or her] heart within him [or her] (*cor*

intus habet) may also be illumined by this light of contemplation.[28]

"To pray is to work, to work is to pray," Eric Gill paraphrases St. Benedict's famous statement, "To pray and to work" (*Ora et labora*). Thus, Saint Benedict charts the way for those who would find spiritual fulfillment in everyday life.

It is within our everyday work life that we must find a way of being prayerful, that we must find our individual and social fulfillment. This position is upheld, as I mentioned, in all traditional cultures. Ananda Coomaraswamy represents the Indian perspective when he states that in traditional society any function (*svadharma*),

> ...however "menial" or "commercial," is strictly speaking a (*marga*) so that it is not by engaging in other work to which a higher or lower social prestige may attach, but to the extent that a man [or a woman] approaches perfection in his [or her] own work and understands its spiritual significance that he [or she] *can rise above himself [or herself]*—an ambition to *rise above his [or her] fellows* having then no longer any real meaning.[29]

Clement of Alexandria (c. 150–c. 215) gives two illustrative examples in his *An Exhortation to the Greeks*: "...Practice husbandry, we say, if you are a husbandman; but while you till your fields, know God. Sail the sea, you who are devoted to navigation, yet call the whilst on the heavenly Pilot...."[30]

Work pervades human endeavor. As humans we are incomplete and unfinished creatures—though some traditions say we are complete, we seem not to recognize our completeness. We therefore have work to do, both outer work—work to "earn a living," keep us alive, function in society—and inner work—work on ourselves. Both inner and outer work comprise "a strange middle kingdom of the human spirit,"[31] occupying that realm between mind and body, between freedom and necessity, and between vision and imagination. "And in this very work, when it is proper work, [humanity] is made teachable. [Humanity] is made humble. [Humanity] is torn open and the derived human spirit is at least prepared to recognize, and to be open to, the

Source of [its] being."[32]

Something in the very process of work can open the possibility for learning and expanded awareness. This "opening" results from a dialectic of sowing and reaping; of asking and receiving; of searching and finding. In truth this "opening" is both the fruit of self-effort and also, the gift of grace. This opening, this being "made teachable," is the object and the subject of a *synergy*; Gregory of Nyssa's term (as well as Maximus') for the interaction of human effort and divine grace in the movement toward deification or perfection. An illustrative image is that of the necessity of two wings on a bird if it is to fly: one wing is human effort, the other wing is divine grace.

WORK IN MONASTIC TRADITION

Christian monasticism has from the first included work in its regimen. Drawing inspiration from scripture, monastics have struggled with the place and function of work within their intentional spiritual communities and within the contemplative life, i.e., the life dedicated and devoted to God. The breadth and depth of experience and insight which the tradition brings to the subject of work and its role in the spiritual life is helpful. In this section I will review a few selected schools of Christian monasticism which have articulated the purposes of work and have addressed the dynamics between inner and outer, contemplation and action, and prayer and work.

The words of St. Benedict provide the best introduction. Chapter 48 of the *Rule of Benedict*, entitled "Daily Manual Labor," contains the critical passage:

> If conditions dictate that they labor in the fields
> (harvesting), they should not be grieved for they are
> truly monks when they must live by manual labor, as
> did our fathers and the apostles. Everything should be
> in moderation, though, for the sake of the timorous.[33]

"The Rule of St. Benedict is extremely detailed in its direction on labor, which it regards as one of the three chief instruments of monastic life," the other two being liturgical prayer and spiritual reading. The Rule legislates minutely on the employment of every hour of the day according to the season of the year: liturgical prayer (Opus Dei) is said seven times each day for a total time of approximately 3 1/2 hours; spiritual reading (scripture or the Fathers) accounts for 2 through 4 hours a day; meals, 1 1/2 hours; sleeping, 8 hours; and manual work 6 1/2 through 7 hours each day.[34]

Monks were to labor either in the fields or the workshops, and every monk took his turn on the kitchen crew (chapter 35). It was also required that all monks work with their hands, old and young, weak and strong, with special consideration given to old and weak (chapter 47). Furthermore, "craftsmen present in the monastery should practice their crafts with humility, as permitted by the abbot" (chapter 57). The spirit of humility, moderation, and balance pervade the Rule. As Owen Chadwick says, "the ascesis which Benedict recommends was spiritual—the ascesis of obedience, humility, patience."[35]

Why the heavy emphasis on manual labor? And why the exacting legislation? First, the overwhelming witness of previous monks included manual labor. From the first and the most influential of them all, St. Antony of the Egyptian desert, monastic life represented an alternating succession of prayer and work (*ora et labora*). Indeed, the Desert Fathers felt manual labor so important that one monk spent all year weaving baskets only to burn them afterwards, in order not to be idle!

A choice story exemplifying the humor in the teachings of the desert is that of Abbot Silvanus who put a monk, one that wanted to be a pure contemplative like Mary the sister of Martha, to reading in his cell, while the others went to work. The monk came out at meal time and asked about getting something to eat. Silvanus said: "Thou art a spiritual man and dost not hold food to be necessary; but we being carnal have need to eat and to that end we work; but thou hast chosen that good part. For thou readest all day and hast no wish for carnal food."[36]

Pachomian monasteries of Egypt refused to accept anyone who would not work. In Cappadocia, St. Basil had a strict obligation of manual labor in his rule: monks who would not work or learn psalms by heart were to be expelled from the community. Both Cassian and Augustine quote the Apostle Paul, "If any [person] will not work, neither let him [or her] eat."

St. Benedict carries on the tradition of making manual work a central aspect of monastic life, with one difference. While he keeps the idea of service (in the service of God, the Opus Dei), "in striking contrast...to his predecessors, Benedict eliminates practically all reference to the contemplative life or the vision of God." His only reference to this is in the Prologue when he says, "...that we may deserve to see Him who has called us."[37] The importance of this difference pertains to the age-old debate about the priority of the active or the contemplative life; between the lay and the religious; between secular and sacred or monastic. Benedict very nearly does away with "...such a double standard."[38]

Be that as it may, Benedict concerned himself with the lives of his monks, and not with establishing a great economic and social power. He legislated manual work, because "idleness is an enemy of the soul" (chapter 48). Besides, his insight into human nature told him that no normal person could spend all their time doing nothing but reading and praying vocally; so, work. In addition, "manual labor was to be no less supernatural than the spiritual reading and prayer which it supplemented."[39]

This supernatural power or quality of labor is related to the individual Christian's striving to live a life of perfection.

> Some form of work was necessary for perfection.... It was not only as an antidote to idleness that the early Christians saw in physical work a means of acquiring individual perfection. They looked upon manual labor as a medium of making reparation for personal sin, a pathway to humility, and an effective method of overcoming concupiscence.[40]

The story of Benedict miraculously retrieving an iron sickle, dropped by a new monk into a lake, and returning it to the unskilled monk with the words, "take it, work on, and do not despair,"[41] is indicative of Benedict's outlook on work. His statement "work on, despair not," especially reveals the monastic attitude in a changing civilization. In contemporary parlance one might hear, "Keep on trucking," or "Keep on, keeping on."

It is important to remember that Benedict structured his monastic community so that the monks lived a life alternating between prayer, study, and work. Many have commented, both ancient and modern, on this closeness and compatibility between work and prayer. St.

Augustine encouraged the union of the two: "As for divine songs, they (the monks) can easily, even while working with their hands, say them, and as though with a divine boat-song cheer up their very toil." He continues with the question, "What then hinders a servant of God while working with his [or her] hands to meditate on the law of the Lord, and to sing to the Name of the Lord Most High?"[42] When work is done in such a manner for such a cause it "...almost ceases to be work...and the line between work and prayer becomes razor thin."[43]

For St. Basil there is no conflict between St. Paul's two instructions, "Pray without ceasing" (1 Thessalonians 5:17) and "You ought to imitate us...we work night and day" (2 Thessalonians 3:8). "Both should be combined," says St. Basil, for "thus, there is an appointed time for prayer, another for labor.... Accordingly, no monk may dispense with labor under pretext of prayer and chant. On the contrary, work itself should be a prayer of praise and thanksgiving reverently rendered to God who has bestowed on man [and woman] the faculties of work and the means of exercising these faculties."[44] This "spiritualizing" of labor not only draws a razor-thin line between prayer and work (*ora et labora*), it also fuses another dimension to work which today is often separated: worship. In addition, to compound this dynamic fusion, intimately bound to worship and work is the idea of service.

Throughout the history of the early church Christians, both lay and clergy, were urged to, in Paul's words, "whatever your task, work heartily, as serving the Lord and men [and women]..." (Colossians 3:23, RSV). The sense of work as worship and as service to God and to Jesus were pervasive. Our modern society stands in stark contrast to such a perspective. It is no wonder then that we moderns have such difficulty appreciating the ascetic purpose of work espoused by monasticism.

St. John Cassian, discussing the life of Egyptian monks, tells us that "giving themselves no rest from work, neither do they ever cease meditation.... It would be tedious to enquire whether it is meditation which permits them to consecrate themselves fully to work, or the other way round—constant work which allows them to progress in the ways of the spirit."[45]

Work and pray unceasingly, such is the regimen of monastic life. Always either at work or at prayer a monk is kept from idleness, for as Benedict emphatically states in the first sentence of his chapter on daily manual labor, "idleness is an enemy of the soul." Augustine comments that a working monk was too occupied to indulge in idle and corrupt discourse.[46] St. Basil includes the ascetic purpose of manual work for the very reasons Benedict states: idleness is harmful and sinful.

"According to Cassian, indolence is a fundamental vice from which many other evils spring."[47] The whole of Book 10 in his *Institutes* contains material on the ascetic purpose of work. The following illustrations from Book 10 are illuminating.

> The cause of all these ulcers, which spring from the root of idleness, he (Paul) heals by a single salutary charge to work. (10,14)[48]

> The wise Fathers of Egypt would in no way suffer the monks and especially the younger to be idle, measuring the state of their heart and their progress in patience and humility by their steadiness at work.... There was a saying approved by the ancient Fathers of Egypt that a busy monk is besieged by a single devil, but an idle one destroyed by spirits innumerable. (10,23)[49]

This last comment is followed by the story of Abbot Paul who wove baskets daily in his cell, even though he lived too far from the market to sell the products of his labor, and "...when his cave would be filled with the work of a whole year, he would set fire to it and burn each year the work he so carefully wrought." (10,24) Of course, as even Dom Sorg comments, "no one [today] thinks of imitating the actions of this holy man, but it is a good illustration of the ascetic necessity of manual labor."[50] Cassian concludes from the story:

> Thereby he (Abbot Paul) proved that without working with his hands a monk cannot endure to abide in his place, nor can he climb any nearer the summit of holiness; and though necessity of making a livelihood in no way demands it, let it be done for the sole purging of the heart, the steadying of thought, perseverance in the cell, and the conquest and final overthrow

of *accidie*[51] itself.
(10,24)

CONCLUSION

It is significant to highlight the monastic understanding and role of work, because we see that very early on people have grappled with the dilemmas and tensions in that intersection of the contemplative and the active, of the inner and the outer, and of prayer and work.

Having defined spirituality, and having shown the importance and the inter-relatedness of the aspects and requirements of a dynamic spirituality, let us now proceed to explore three other areas of work, worship, service, and attitude, that major figures in the monastic tradition of Christian history have incorporated as solutions to these dilemmas and tensions.

3

THE ART OF WORKING

Where there is artistic excellence there is human
dignity.
>   Maori exhibit, DeYoung Museum

That lyf so short, the craft so long to lerne.
>   Geoffrey Chaucer

Some early monastics and theologians reflect on the phenomenon
of work, especially manual work, through the lenses of worship, service, and attitude. There is an "art of working," though amorphous and
elusive, which lies within the scope of these three lenses.

Let us begin by analyzing the views of William Morris, Eric Gill,
and Dorothy Sayers, three Britons, each highly reflective about craft
and aesthetics.

William Morris[1] was an avowed disciple of John Ruskin who,
among other things, attempted in his writings "...to weld economics
and aesthetics into a gospel of work."[2] In opposition to most artists
Morris objected to the separation of the fine from the useful arts,
believing that people must live in fellowship and have joy in their
work or they will perish.

Eric Gill's[3] life journey cannot be separated from his artistic journey. His pursuits were aimed at establishing a "cell of good living," as
he called it. He believed fervently in the "priesthood of craftsmanship"
and strove throughout his life, indeed *with* his life and his art, to re-
animate the freedom and responsibility of men and women inherent
in artisanship, i.e., quality work and art. In addition to sculpting, Gill
was an accomplished wood engraver and typographer/calligrapher.

His journey included a conversion to Roman Catholicism and engagement with the social movement known as Distributism. Gill was

also a prolific writer, reflecting on aesthetics and work, and also on theology. Finding much of his fundamental material in medieval art and theology, Gill was an anomally among artists, harkening to past days and traditional ways of doing and thinking; he was nevertheless a perceptive and demanding critic and a prolific and recognized artist.

Dorothy Sayers'[4] reflections on aesthetics and work, like those of Gill and Morris, draw upon the traditional understanding that persons (humanity) are the point of work and of the economy. And, like Gill and Morris, she finds the meaning of work in the work itself. She calls for "...a thorough-going revolution in our whole attitude to work."[5] Work should be seen "...not as a necessary drudgery..., but as a way of life in which the nature of [humanity] should find its proper experience and delight and so fulfill itself to the glory of God."[6]

Why do we usually not consider work as art? We consider art to be fine quality work; why not the reverse? When work tends to be considered drudgery, to be completed as quickly as possible, in order that we can get on with living, it lacks quality and any semblance of art. Workers often invest little energy, skill and care in the activity or the product. Rather, work is viewed as distasteful and as an obstacle to living "the good life." Workers often are not making the things themselves but are merely minding machines which do the making, or they are "making" only a piece of the final product. Indeed, the product belongs to someone else, for workers do not own, in the vast majority of cases, the product of their work.

In order, therefore, to enhance the concern of workers for the quality of their work one must find ways for workers (1) to enjoy their work, (2) to have a genuine part in the production of the product, and (3) to have ownership and control of their work: both the process and the product.

Artists usually find satisfaction in their work, often make the entire piece themselves, and own that which they create. Even if the piece is commissioned, an artist's work is his/hers; an artist trades or contracts to create the piece of art in exchange for money or some other form of payment. The artist's control or ownership is inherent in the source of the product, i.e., himself or herself; his or her creative skill in manifesting an idea.

ART AND QUALITY

Removing the Plate of the Pump
on the Hydraulic System
of the Backhoe

for Burt Hybart

Through mud, fouled nuts, black grime
it opens, a gleam of spotless steel
machined-fit perfect
swirl of intake and output
relentless clarity
at the heart
of work.

Gary Snyder[7]

Now let us discuss the ramifications of quality upon the worker himself or herself and, to a limited extent, upon the workplace itself.

The question is, how to help workers gain concern for the quality of their work. The answer fundamentally resides in transforming workers into artists concerned with the quality of their work.

Dorothy Sayers says the workers' first duty is to serve the work rather than a sense of community, for community service tends to change over time or to lead to expectations of something in return. To serve the work itself is a matter of doing good work, i.e., quality work. Good work does not result from piety in the worker or from some pose of being a good and/or a "religious" person.

> No piety in the worker will compensate for work that is not true to itself; for work that is untrue to its own technique is a living lie...the living and eternal truth is expressed in work only in so far as that work is true in itself, to itself, to the standards of its own technique ...work must be good work before it can call itself God's work.[8]

Quality work is its own reward; "...the satisfaction of beholding its perfection." Indeed, "the work takes all and gives nothing but itself; and to serve the work is a labour of pure love."[9]

A major argument against those who would improve the quality of work life and who seek to find ways by which working people may find dignity, interest, and pleasure in their work, is that people will always have to work, often at hard physical labor. However, there is, as William Morris articulates, a difference between "useful work" and "useless toil." The difference being that the "one has hope in it, the other has not." The nature of this hope is three-fold: hope of rest; hope of product; and hope of pleasure in the work itself.[10] Morris states the distinction as "rough labour" verses degrading and unpleasurable labour.

"Rough labour" is necessary to the work of the world. Degrading labour, on the other hand, is "the toil which makes the thousand and one things which nobody wants, which are used merely as the counters for the competitive buying and selling, falsely called commerce." Useless toil pleads to be done away with. For Morris, this reform can be brought about only through art.[11]

By "art" I mean the making of things with a "high quality of conception or execution," following *The American Heritage Dictionary*'s fourth definition of the word. Art is, as this definition implies, first and foremost, a state or reflection of mind. In other words, the work of art originates in the mind of the artist, whether it be via insight, revelation, or another mode of conception. In addition, there is a level of skill involved in this conception, for the "thought" must be made tangible for it to be art. There is, therefore, an effort required on the part of the person involved in conceiving this art; the artist must actively participate in the creation. Through "...the intentional focusing of sufficiently disciplined and directed energy upon the dream..."[12] a work of art is realized.

A work of art is a word made flesh! It is the interaction of mind and something tangible created through human work.

The "art of working" is important in relationship to the concept of the spirituality of work, for art demands a sense of quality and calls for a certain attitude from the artist. Both Eric Gill and Dorothy Sayers claim "art is the making of something well."[13] Art involves skill and a certain vision, a mental image of the end product. In a sense, the Incarnation is the greatest work of art.

Because art is "making something well," quality is decisive to the

artistic-ness of an object. An artist does not throw just anything together and call it art. By the very use of the words "artist" and "art" we
imply a concern with quality. A piece of art or an act of art is something in which we recognize skill and concern for making or doing it
well.

"The artist is not a special kind of person, but every person is a
special kind of artist."[14] But we have lost much of our artful dimension
because we are alienated from our work, from ourselves, from our
neighbors, and from nature. While it may seem ludicrous to equate
artists and working people, it is necessary to reshape our attitudes and
actions toward, and in, the work-a-day world. Workers as artists will
gain a concern for the quality of their work and will find fulfillment
and happiness in their work. Our modern industrialized society has
accomplished something "never before achieved in the whole history
of the world;"[15] the division of artist from workman/woman, a split
now totally taken for granted.

In an address, "Art and Its Producers," delivered in Liverpool, England, before the National Association for the Advancement of Art in
1888, William Morris gave a superb description of the attitude and
spirit required in production in order for the product to be considered
a work of art.

> ...the integrity and sincerity of this...art...depends
> on the wares of which it forms a part being produced
> by craftsmanship, for the use of persons who under-
> stand craftsmanship. ...The carpenter makes a chest
> for the goldsmith one day, the goldsmith a cup for the
> carpenter on another, and there is sympathy in their
> work.... *Each is conscious during his work of making a
> thing to be used by a man of like needs to himself....*
> done in the spirit I have told you of, they will inevita-
> bly be works of art. In work so done there is and must
> be the interchange of interest in the occupation of
> life; the knowledge of human necessities and the con-
> sciousness of human goodwill is a part of all such
> work, and the world is linked together by it.[16]

Art and artisanship are forms of work still viable and necessary for
the reintegration of personality and for reinvesting work with dignity,

skill and quality.[17] This involves both the aesthetics of the workplace itself and the aesthetics of the finished product. "All things made could be, and should be, regarded as we regard the products of artists."[18]

For Morris, the *Aim of Art* is to increase the happiness of people "...in short, to make [humanity's] work happy and [our] rest fruitful."[19] Morris sees a direct connection between industrial slavery, which he labels "proletarianization," and the degradation of the arts. For him, art—both the attitude and the practice of—is the saving grace. Art destroys the curse of labour "...by making work the pleasurable satisfaction of our impulse towards energy, and giving to that energy hope of producing something worth its exercise."[20]

The key to finding this happiness, destroying the curse of labor, and being an artist in whatever one's work, according to Morris, is found in taking a sincere interest in all the details of daily life. This, he says, we can only do by raising them through art.

Everyone can be an artist, for everyone does some work and must attend to the details of daily life. It is only when the curse or burden of the necessities of "making a living" drive one to exhaustion and irresponsibility ("proletarianization" in Morris' terminology) that those daily details become superfluous and debilitating. Through control over one's work and life this attention to daily details can once again become the liberating vehicle and path for workers. By taking an interest in all the details of daily life people not only can gain control over their lives but will also begin to experience pleasure in their labor. This last quality—the taking pleasure in labor—is the opening to "real art" according to Morris.

Eric Gill does not hold work to be of an intrinsically good nature. He believes that work is a curse and always has been, and that until modern industrialization the curse has been alleviated by art. He sees problems today due to (1) having separated art and work, and (2) misunderstandings about humanity, that is, about the kind of creature humanity is.

MEANS AND ENDS

The experience of quality in work itself is not possible in our present system which views work as "...an evil, [in which] individual liberty means liberty to emancipate one's self from work, and that whatever pays best is right...."[21] Such a system denies the two sources of real wealth: (1) the fruit of the earth, and (2) the labour of people.[22] In our system of industrialist capitalism it is impossible to realistically appraise work for our reasoning, and hence our priorities, are backwards. This reversal of priorities is clearly apparent from a Christian perspective. "The real estimate of work is not the money it brings to the producer, but...the worth of the thing that is made." The work itself is the value, not the money.[23]

From a Christian perspective, as opposed to the reigning but "wholly false and pagan understanding of work,"[24] work is natural to humanity. Implications for everyday practice are substantial. First, it is implied that "work is not primarily a thing one does to live, but the thing one lives to do." Seen in this light, we can agree with Sayers that "work should be the medium in which the worker offers him [or her] self to God."[25] Second, it is implied that the secular vocation is sacred; each person must be able to serve God *in* his or her work, and, the work itself must be acceptable and respected as the medium of divine creation. It is *within* each worker's profession, not outside it, that he or she is called to serve God. Third, it is implied that the workers' first duty is to serve the work itself.

One might argue that these premises do not address the world as it really is, and do not take into account the hard economic realities central to any realistic discussion of work today. While the details of our economic situation may be different today than they were 40 years ago, the underlying realities and the fundamental issues of work are no different: "The economic solution will not solve this problem, because it is not really an economic problem at all, but a problem about human nature and the nature of work."[26] Indeed, it is a spiritual problem!

We have become confused by mixing up the ends to which our work is aimed with the way in which the work is done. For "the end of the work will be decided by our religious outlook: as we are so we make."[27] Eric Gill echoes Sayers' sentiments: "Everything depends upon the nature of the end desired and ends are many and various."[28]

Our confusion rests, fundamentally, on the inversion of priorities concerning the meaning and purpose of human life. The modernized western world[29] no longer follows the religious and traditional understandings of humankind's place and role in creation. The modern world has replaced the traditional; we have redefined the goals of human life.

While the "ends are many and various," as Gill says, not all ends are relative or worthwhile. For example, "among the early Christians the desire of money was held to be the root of all evil; today, that desire is instilled into every schoolboy and girl. This may be right or wrong, but it cannot be called the same."[30]

I believe the world's religious traditions hold the key to the meaning and purpose of human life. The ends may be expressed differently by different traditions, but there is a commonality in essentials: the end of humanity is "to know thy Self" or "to know God."

The modern secular world is racing headlong in pursuit of very different goals; goals, however, which are neither original nor unique: wealth, power, property, experience, pleasure. From ancient times the human dilemma persists. And so I claim that this work like all works of those with faith is evangelical in nature and of necessity. In this matter I am in full agreement with Eric Gill that we are all evangelists and that all of our works are in essence evangelical, that is, that their object or end is the securing of happiness.

This mixing-up of the ends of human life, as well as that to which our work is put, is the result of many influences. The consequences in the world of work are devastating.

Alienation is a term often used to describe our modern predicament. Karl Marx states in his *Economic and Philosophical Manuscripts* (1844) the classical definition of alienation:

> In what does the alienation of labor consist? First, that the work is external to the worker, that it is not a part of his [or her] nature, that consequently he [or she] does not fulfill him [or her] self in his [or her] work but denies him [or her] self, has a feeling of misery, not of wellbeing....The worker therefore feels himself [or herself] at home only during his [or her] leisure, whereas at work he [or she] feels homeless.[31]

A vivid portrayal of factory work, reflecting such alienation, is given by Antler in his poem "Factory," a few stanzas of which follow:

And I know that in one day owning this place

I'd make more than if my life worked my lifetime here.

....

How many watching me watch the woman
teach me my job
Remembered *their* first day on the job,
Remembered wondering what the woman felt
teaching them in a minute
the work she'd done all her life,
Showing them so fast all they needed to know?

....

So nothing called life can torment you with undertak-
ings
and your only responsibility toward mankind is to
check for defects in the ends of cans.[32]

Two reasons for this alienation are (1) industrialism and the factory system itself, and (2) the institution of private property. Quotes
from Eric Gill and Harry Ward illustrate these two viewpoints.
Gill states that "the factory system is unChristian because:

It puts the service and glory of man[sic] before the
service and glory of God.
It promotes the comfort of man[sic] and destroys the
worship and praise of God.
It puts the making of money before the making of
goods.
It puts quantity before quality.

....

It deprives the workman of responsibility for his [or
her] work.
It is subject only to "efficient causes" and not to
"final causes"

....

It subdivides labour so that a workman becomes
merely a tool.
It puts a premium upon mechanical dexterity and a
discount upon intellectual and spiritual ability in
the workman.

....

It depends upon militarism....
It promotes wars, for it destroys local markets and
    makes trade dependent upon "world markets" and
    financial magnates. Over-production is inevitable and
    when there is overproduction there must be a
    struggle for fresh markets.[33]

A North American clergyman and social ethicist, Professor Harry
F. Ward's critique of private property is well summarized in the following quotation from *Our Economic Morality and the Ethic of Jesus*:

The shorter catechism used to teach children that the
chief end of man [and woman] is "to glorify God and
to enjoy [God] forever." But the heirs of the makers of
the acquisitive society are instructed from infancy that
the most important business of life is to get property
and pass it on to one's descendants, to have and to
hold forever....For such persons the guiding star to
conduct is the fixed idea that man's [and woman's] life
consists in the abundance of things he [or she] possesses....If it is the pursuit of profit that calls forth
most of the energies of modern man [and woman],
most of that profit is immediately transformed into
property, for which purpose it is sought. What, then, is
property that it should compete with the experience
of God as the chief end of [Humanity]?[34]

Gill and Ward point to the need of achieving a desired goal, a goal
which calls for both inner and outer work. Here, dealing with both the
process and the outcome or product of work, we remember that work
occurs both inside and outside, and realize how crucial a person's attitude is. Furthermore, having seen the relation of art to the production
of quality work we are conscious of the important role art plays in
realizing the appropriate ends, through the appropriate means.
    The conjunction of inner and outer work, understood within the
realm of means and ends, and as it manifests in peoples' everyday
work lives, needs to be spoken of in terms of craftsmanship or artisanship.

CRAFT AND ATTITUDE

The following story about three masons illustrates the difference made by our attitude toward work.

Upon visiting a construction site, a reporter asked three brick masons what they were doing. The first answered gruffly, "I'm laying bricks." The second replied, "I'm earning my week's pay." But the third mason said enthusiastically and with obvious pride, "I'm building a cathedral."

We see here how a person's attitude toward work can dramatically effect his or her very personality. The same task may have entirely different effects upon the character of the worker, according to the spirit in which it is done.

Craft implies a certain attitude toward one's work and toward one's self. As Carla Needleman, a North American craftsperson, writes in her book, *The Work of Craft*, a true craftsperson is "...led, thanks to the craft, thanks to the discoveries about [my]self that the craft is presenting me with, along a path of self-knowledge...."[35]

Seeing work as craftsmanship involves enlarging the scope of work beyond the traditional "crafts" of pottery, weaving, wood, and metal/jewelry. Work as craft can be a spiritual path. The working artisan's "...efforts in the medium of his [or her] craft, to bring about a right understanding in him [or her] self, a way of right action, his [or her] groping efforts toward understanding and expressing something true in the objects they produce, little by little bring about a transformation in the crafts[person] him [or her] self." And *here is the link*, the core of the connection with work, art and spirituality: "This transformation of attitude is itself the channel of connection with the larger world."[36]

Carla Needleman continues, intertwining question, goal, and means as elements in this transformation of attitude. Indeed, the dynamics are such that "...the transformation of the attitude of the crafts[person] is a transformation of the crafts[person] him [or her] self."[37]

> A question, like an aim, is a direction and a kind of signpost. The question and the attitude that supports it are the thoroughfare of the goal, the way of the goal. An aim has to partake of the attitude of the goal

itself. The goal determines the means. It is even more
intimate than that, less differentiated. The means are
the atmosphere of the goal, the very emanations of
the goal. The aim and what is seen as the goal, seen
with partial vision as a far-off fixed point, are essentially the same, of the same "stuff." Therefore, the
transformation of the attitude of the crafts[person] is
a transformation of the crafts[person] him [or her]self.
It affects him [or her] even in his [or her] postures,
even in the degree of his [or her] physical relaxation.
It is, though he [or she] might not just then realize it,
the channel that connects him [or her]. His [or her]
aim, his [or her] deepest question, his [or her] most
heartfelt wish, that which seems to originate most
personally and directly only from himself [or herself],
comes as well from another level of being, calling to
the place in him [or her] that echoes it.[38]

Needleman expresses the mood of many contemporary craftspeople. The "new craftsperson" strives to overcome the separation between process and product. In this struggle we see efforts to transcend the distinction the Greeks made between labor and work. The
new craftsperson consummates a marriage of the two seemingly disparate modes of being. Artisans, people previously or traditionally
involved only with process, are becoming artists, involved with actual-
izing a product. What we see in this marriage of craftspersons and
artists,[39] and also of workers and artists, is the attempt to manifest or
incarnate the realization of the truth that the means and the ends are
one.

While in the political world the end is never reached and one is
always in the midst of the means, in the work world crafts do material-
ize into finished products. The process dictates the form of the product: good workmanship produces good products while poor workmanship produces poor products.

Gandhi and other exponents of non-violent resistance point to
the reality of the never-ending process of means in which the "end" is
never reached, the focus remains on the means of getting where they
want to go. Likewise the new craftspeople recognize the dual importance of the creative process and the created product.

And so it is with those on the spiritual path: the quality of the journey determines the destination. Here we are in the realm of the *art of living*!

Here the process of living determines the outcome of a person's life, an understanding different from that of Arendt. It is not what a person *does* per se, but who and what a person *is*. Interestingly enough Arendt is in agreement if the discussion is limited to art. She, however, misses the opportunity to move the work verses labor discussion to a higher plane by not making the connection between work and art, for in the context of "art" Arendt comments that greatness is correctly derived from what one *is* rather than from what one *does*.[40] Her statement begs the question, "If that is the case for artists, why not for workers?"

Even if we cannot agree whether a person is defined by what one does or what one is, it is clearly in the interplay of the two that personality is molded and realized.

Today what we are making is *ourselves*. We are the raw material (body, mind, and spirit) with which we form and mold, plant and water, *in order to make a new being*. Through our work on ourselves we are working a transformation of our being. *We* are the *workshop* in which God's creation is "brought round right," to quote the Quaker song. It is in and through us human beings that the consubstantial union of matter and spirit is forged—through the fire of pleasure and pain, of struggle and growth—into the whole and free persons which we are meant and called to be.

We are at the center of the universe. In truth, we *are* the center of the universe. And, as such, it is in and through us and the life we live that God's creation can find fulfillment. All of creation is redeemed through life, death, and resurrection. The process, how we live our lives, who and what we make of ourselves, is what accomplishes the end product.

I close this section with the following poem, adapted from *The Way of Chang Tzu* by Thomas Merton, which portrays with crystal clarity the place of attitude in making work fulfilling.

The Wood Carrier

Khing, the master carver, made a bell stand
Of precious wood. When it was finished,

All who saw it were astounded. They said it
  must be
The work of spirits.
The Prince of Lu said to the master carver:
"What is your secret?"

Khing replied: "I am only a workman:
I have no secret. There is only this:
When I began to think about the work you
  commanded
I guarded my spirit, did not expend it
On trifles, that were not to the point.
I fasted in order to set
My heart at rest.
After three days fasting,
I had forgotten gain and success.
After five days
I had forgotten praise or criticism.
After seven days
I had forgotten my body
With all its limbs.

"By this time all thought of your Highness
And of the court had faded away.
All that might distract me from the work
Had vanished.
I was collected in the single thought
of the bell stand.

"Then I went to the forest
To see the trees in their own natural state.
When the right tree appeared before my eyes,
The bell stand also appeared in it, clearly,
  beyond doubt.
All I had to do was to put forth my hand
And begin.

"If I had not met this particular tree
There would have been

No bell stand at all.

"What happened?
My own collected thought
Encountered the hidden potential in the wood;
From this live encounter came the work.
Which you ascribe to the spirits."[41]

With this poem Chang Tzu and Merton also introduce the issue of detachment.

DETACHMENT

Invariably, for most people in today's active world, problems and misunderstandings arise regarding the disposition or quality of detachment or disinterestedness. The very idea rankles the modern mind. "How can you really be concerned about the world if you are detached from it?" "How can you be true to your real feelings and needs, let alone know yourself, if you are detached?" "How can you have art if you are detached from life?" We can hear the ad-infinitum cacophony of outraged sensibility from a world committed to being "connected," "concerned," and "involved" in and with the world.

The notion of detachment and of actively seeking the state of detachment is incredibly foreign to our modern way of thinking. And yet, detachment is a central component in the spiritual paths of all religious traditions. Detachment is a Hindu term. Equivalent terms from other traditions are *apatheia*, from early Christian contemplatives; *emptiness*, from Buddhism; *Abgeschiedenheit* or indifference, from Meister Eckhardt; and *sobriety*, from the Sufi tradition.[42]

An illuminating source on detachment from the vast treasury of Indian culture is the *Bhagavad Gita*, from which the following two quotations are taken.

The world becomes bound by action unless it be done
for the sake of Sacrifice. Therefore, O son of Kunti,
give up attachment and do your work for the sake of
the Lord. (3.9)[43]

Therefore always do without attachment the work you
have to do; for a [person] who does [their] work without attachment attains the Supreme. (3.19)[44]

Continuing in this line of thought, Swami Vivekananda, a leading
light of the Hindu renaissance of the late 19th and early 20th centuries states in his book *Karma Yoga*:

We read in the Bhagavad-Gita again and again that
we must all work incessantly. All work is by nature
composed of good and evil. We cannot do any work
which will not do some good somewhere; there cannot
be any work which will not cause some harm somewhere. Every work must necessarily be a mixture of
good and evil; yet we are commanded to work incessantly. Good and evil will both have their results, will
produce their Karma. Good action will entail upon us
good effect; bad actions, bad. But good and bad are
both bondages of the soul. The solution reached in
the Gita in regard to this bondage-producing nature of
work is, that if we do not attach ourselves to the work
we do, it will not have any binding effect on our soul.
We shall try to understand what is meant by this "non-
attachment" to work....

...If you can invariably take the position of a giver, in
which everything given by you is a free offering to the
world without any thought of return, then will your
work bring you no attachment. Attachment comes
only where we expect a return.[45]

That which is valuable and, indeed, essential, about detachment is
its connection to our striving to overcome the inherent tension
between contemplation and action. It is a quality of being, a countenance pervading the personality. Swami Vivekananda describes this
countenance well:

The ideal [person] is he [or she] who in the midst of

the greatest silence and solitude finds the intensest
[sic] activity, and in the midst of the intensest [sic]
activity finds the silence and solitude of the desert.[46]

Relating detachment to the world of work, Vivekananda says, "...This
is the ideal of Karma-Yoga; and if you have attained to that, you have
really learnt the secret of work."[47]

How so, "the secret of work"?: As the answer to the riddle of
bringing heaven down to earth where we all live; of finding spiritual
fulfillment in daily life! Non-attachment (the term Vivekananda uses
for detachment) is a state attainable by any one, it is not exclusive to
monks. Indeed, Vivekananda and other exponents of Hinduism are
clear that the life of the householder is just as adequate a station for
the spiritual life as anywhere.

It is useless to say that the [person] who lives out of
the world is a greater [person] than he [or she] who
lives in the world; it is much more difficult to live in
the world and worship God than to give it up and live
a free and easy life.[48]

The question regarding detachment, non-attachment, disinterestedness, etc., is not whether you or I like or dislike, agree or disagree,
but, rather, what is it that such a state or countenance "gets" at? What
does detachment engender? What does it allow or call forth from a
person? Why do all the traditions consider detachment so central in
the spiritual life? It will not do for us—modern readers and search-
ers—to simply discard such a state (or idea) of being because it does
not "fit" or agree with our conceptual apparatus or our emotional
and/or volitional disposition and criteria.

Both artists and mystics speak of the importance of detachment.
Statements from two artists who have addressed the issue, are insight-
ful. First, Ben Shahn writes in *The Shape of Content*:

The artist...must maintain an attitude at once detached and deeply involved. Detached, in that he [or
she] must view all things with an outer and abstracting
eye....Whoever would know [their] day or would

capture its essential character must maintain such a degree of detachment.

But besides perceiving these things, the artist must also feel them. Therein he [or she] differs from the scientist, who may observe dispassionately, collate, draw conclusions, and still remain uninvolved. The artist may not use line or colors or forms unless he [or she] is able to feel their rightness....So, he [or she] must never fail to be involved in the pleasures and the desperations of [human]kind....[49]

Second, Eric Gill, in "Art and Holiness" states:

The disinterestedness of the artist, the maker, the responsible workman is the thing which makes him [or her] friend and brother [sic] to the saint, the holy [person]. The saint is the disinterested man [or woman]; the artist is the disinterested workman [woman]. Their disinterestedness is their common ground....[50]

Being detached does not necessarily imply a stolid and somber attitude. Indeed, we see in Gill how gaiety is an integral part of such art and work:

Religion is the experience of God. Religious art is the work of people experiencing themselves as God—"I have said ye are gods." Holiness is the fruit of religion. The holy person sees him [or herself] whole, and gaiety is the mark of holiness. Holiness and therefore gaiety are the marks of religious art. "Be you also holy"—that is the whole law and the prophets.[51]

Can one be gay and not sing!

I hear America singing, the varied carols I hear,
Those of mechanics, each one singing his as it should
    be

blithe and strong,
The carpenter singing his as he measures his plank
   or beam,
The mason singing his as he makes ready for work,
   or leaves off work,
The boatman singing what belongs to him in
   his boat, the deck-hand singing on the steamboat
   deck,
The shoemaker singing as he sits on his bench,
   the hatter singing as he stands,
The wood-cutter's song, the ploughboy's on his way in
   the morning,
or at noon intermission or at sundown,
The delicious singing of the mother, or of the young
   wife at work,
or of the girl sewing or washing,
Each singing what belongs to him or her and to none
   else,
The day what belongs to the day—at night the party of
   young fellows,
robust, friendly,
Singing with open mouths their strong melodious
   songs.

> "I Hear America Singing" (1860–67)
> Walt Whitman[52]

But America no longer sings. Working people no longer sing. No longer is "each singing what belongs to him or her and to none else."[53] There is something wrong when we no longer sing at our work, in our work, for our work. The work, and the society which gives birth to and sustains it, has become besotted. It has lost its soul, its soul-giving and soul-building qualities.

It is not enough to call for ways to adapt ourselves to the changing world of work. We must—if we would recapture the ability to sing —change the nature of work. We must adapt the work to us!

To regain our dignity, our human-ness, therefore, involves new and different attitudes toward life and work. It involves learning to sing again. In the work-a-day world this manifests itself through working worshipfully.

Summarizing well the worshipful quality of work possible through detachment, Vivekananda states:

> God allows us to work. It's blasphemy to think we are "helping" God....We are here at God's pleasure. WE can not help; what we do (should do!) is worship. ...God is all in all. We are allowed to worship God. Stand in that reverent attitude to the whole universe, and then will come perfect non-attachment. This should be your duty. This is the proper attitude of work. This is the secret taught by Karma-Yoga.[54]

WORSHIP

Sanctification, holiness, deification, perfection, union with God: these are terms for the purpose of human life, for the end toward which we all strive, either consciously or unconsciously. Theophan the Recluse states that we must "work with our hands and yet remain with God in mind and heart."[55] This is worship. So, too, from the monastics we learn of the importance of integrating work and prayer.

> Benedict did not first ask whether a brother were competent in his craft or brought material benefit to the monastery by his work, but whether what he did served to glorify God or his own ego. If anyone did not have the spirit of humility, his entire work was worthless in the eyes of the holy patriarch....What is said "of the craftsmen" applies to every occupation....Where God's glory is sought in labor, and all activity is motivated by the intention of serving God in true dedication, the results of labor are lasting....For St. Benedict work too was a religious service, an *Opus Dei*, labor for God, and came under the heading: "U.I.O.G.D.: *Ut in omnibus glorificetur Deus*: That in all things God may be glorified." For St. Benedict work was never an end in itself. It must be fitted into the sublime over-all

purpose of life: to attain to God by means of the "Lord's service"....[56]

Dom Rembert Sorg, O.S.B., in his book *Towards a Benedictine Theology of Manual Labor*, illustrates the relationship between prayer and work with the parable of "...a man who took his plow and went out into his fields saying: 'I am going to plant some *Matins* and *Lauds* for the family.'"[57] In further clarification Sorg continues:

> ...the farmer in the parable...lives an integrated life that is knit together by unity and spirit and love. He feeds his cows and it is a singing of Lauds; he cleans his barn and it is a love of God and of neighbor sprung into act; for the end and purpose specify the work. In the very image and likeness of God he asserts his true dignity and aristocracy as the lord of creation, and his animals and tools and meadows and fields and machines sing with him.[58]

Another illustration of this relationship is from St. Jerome who, in recalling his time among the monks at Bethlehem, describes the monks' lives in this manner:

> ...Whithersoever you turn, the farmer holding his plough-handle sings an Alleluia; the sweating reaper diverts himself with psalms and the vine-dresser, pruning the vine with his curved sickle sings something Davidic. These are the songs in this province; these, in common parlance, are the love ballads; this is the shepherd's whistling; these are the implements of culture.[59]

Though I urge a worshipful style of work, I do not advocate a complete elimination of the balance or rhythm between worship, prayer and work. Arguments by Edward Kaiser and Joseph Pieper[60] convince me of the desirability of maintaining the "holy rhythm of work and prayer."[61] "The relation of work to sacred repose [i.e., worship] is," as Kaiser says, "an inseparable element of divine Revelation and the providential plan for [humanity's] activity in the universe."[62] It is, furthermore, through the celebration of Sunday, in this case, or sacred repose, that work and the rest of the work week are sanctified. Thus, work becomes consecrated insofar as people recognize the sovereignty of God.

Continuing Kaiser's thinking, we realize that if work is directed to worship, work is not ultimate but a means toward the end of union with God. Indeed, "without the sacred time of repose and worship [humanity] becomes a mere slave of work."[63]

Even if work becomes "art" and "worshipful," it is still necessary to take repose from work. There is a need for alternating rest and exertion if we are not to become slaves of work and if work is not to be made an idol. This is *not* to imply that there is a secular realm opposed to a sacred realm; work and worship do not oppose one another as suggested by systematic theology. Rather, they are two complementary poles in human existence.

Festivity in worship is also a necessary part of being human. It may alternate with daily work, but festivity may not be eliminated if we are to remain whole and healthy. Worship, including festivity, and work are the two wings required for flight; just as the holy bird flies with wings of grace and effort. The "holy rhythm" of work and worship is akin to the consubstantiality of matter and spirit in that work and worship are inter-related and necessary for full human living.

Douglas Steere tells of the failure of a meditation center which had good facilities, pleasant climate, tasty food, but insubstantial activity and work for the participants:

> A redemptive outlet [to draw] some corner of the yearning, toiling creation up with them....[T]hey could not bear, nor could they absorb, this concentration of worship [3–5 hours a day of prayer] without being more deeply engaged in works of charity whether in hard work in garden or household, in hospital work, in teaching, or even in writing. Without this connection, the worship, the contemplation, seemed to be lacking in redemptive, tendering power. It became unconvincing, and charity declined.[64]

CHARITY OR SELFLESS SERVICE

Charity expresses love in the service of neighbor. As Kahlil Gibran remarks, "Work is love made visible."

> Man [sic] is a social animal. [We are] not self-suffi-cient. [We] cannot live without [our] neighbors; they cannot live without [us]. But the object of life is "your sanctification." Therefore all our neighborliness must have that end in view, and therefore we are all evan-gelists and all our works are in their true nature evan-gelical; they have for their object, their final cause, their end, the winning of beatitude.[65]

The "integrality" of humanity, to use Gill's term, is once again apparent: work, evangelism, happiness, worship link together bound by selfless service.

In his letter to the church at Colossia the apostle Paul says, "Whatever you do, work at it from the heart as for the Lord and not for men, knowing that from the Lord you will receive the inheritance as your reward. Serve the Lord Christ."[66] We are to regard our labor as a service to God and a gift to God. For the works of men and women carry the work of creation on to a higher

> ...level than that of what we call Nature. We are our-selves creators. Through us exist things which God Himself [sic] could not otherwise have made....Our works are [God's] works, but they are also in a strict sense our own, and if we present them to [God] they are *our* presents to [God], and not simply [God's] to [God's]self. They are free-will offerings. And, indeed, all things should thus be offered up.[67]

The early fathers and the monastic founders are nearly unanimous in their view of work, especially manual work, as fundamental to a life of love and charity. The purpose of work is to provide for the self-support of the monks and the monasteries, and the giving of alms.

In keeping with their profession to follow the way of perfection, almsgiving is an obligation of a monk. "For perfection is surely the 'better' thing and 'it is a more blessed thing to give than to receive'."[68] Monks lived under a vow of poverty with no alternative other than work for the providing of alms. "Working to produce alms is the positive life and joyous exercise of monastic poverty. Above all it is the technique of perfect charity."[69]

Paul expresses the principle clearly: "I have shown you all things, how that so laboring you ought to support the weak, and to remember the word of the Lord Jesus, how he said: 'It is a more blessed thing to give rather than to receive'"(Acts 20:35). Jerome comments, "...even supposing that you give all your property to the poor, Christ will value nothing more highly than what you have wrought with your own hands."[70] And from Cassian, "Such assistance should come from the fruits of labor rather than from accumulated supplies or funds."[71] Basil the Great explains that the motive for manual labor is pure charity. He writes in his Rule:

> It has to be understood that the one who works must do so not to supply his own needs by his work, but to fulfill the Lord's command Who said: "I was hungry and you gave me to eat." For to be solicitous for oneself is altogether forbidden by the Lord saying: "Be not solicitous for your life, what you shall eat, nor for your body, what you shall put on," and adding: "For after all these things do the heathens seek." Wherefore, in labor the purpose set before everyone is support of the needy, not one's own necessity. For thus will he avoid the accusation of self-love and he will receive the blessing of brotherly love from the Lord saying: "Whatever you have done to one of my least brethren, you have done to me."[72]

This perspective which integrates work, service, and charity is exactly that of Karma Yoga: the way of action. The quotations earlier in the chapter from the *Baghavad Gita* and Swami Vivekananda exemplify the aims of a karma yogi; the non-attachment and the offering of one's work with no desire for reward. Likewise, karma yoga is "...a way of coming to God through living life as an act of devoted service...."[73] However, as in the Christian tradition, karma yoga also affirms that a person cannot claim heaven or perfection merely by one's works. In the words of Ram Das, a North American karma yogi, "...Hard work alone [is] not the essence of the matter. Rather, it [is] work carried on with remembrance of God; that is, work done with love in the presence of God's grace."[74] We see here the connection between attitude, worship, and service.

With Martin Luther's rediscovery of the New Testament message that every Christian is called into the service of God, the idea of vocation could be applied to all types of work. It no longer mattered what you did for work, as long as it was done for the glory of God. "The difference in value no longer [lay] in the kind of work...done, but simply in its having, or not having, this divine purpose."[75] In other words, "...the valuation of work is shifted from the 'what' to the 'why' and 'how'."[76]

Eric Gill declares that, "...the idea of service is inseparable from the idea of art....No one can buy things that they have not, as they say, 'got a use' for."[77] As an example Gill points out that "the painter renders a service. It is a service of doing in paint what is rightly done in the place where painting should rightly go."[78]

> So it is with all the arts, and the distinction is not be-
> tween art and skill or between art and utility as though
> we were distinguishing between spirit and matter or
> between soul and body; for art and skill are the same
> thing and all arts are in a proper sense useful arts. The
> distinction is simply between those arts which serve
> the body and those which serve the mind.[79]

Work as Dorothy Sayers tells us, "...should be the *medium* in which the worker offers him or her self to God."[80] Thus, work should not be seen as toil but as service. I think Sayers is rather romantic in her view of work, even work as it "should be," but she provides a forthright witness to the importance of holding service and work together. Echoing Luther and the Protestant understanding of vocation Sayers declares that "the secular vocation, as such, is sacred."[81] Consequently, "every maker and worker is called to serve God in their profession or trade—not outside it."[82]

Both work and art are linked to service, not just any service but the service of beauty, use, God, and neighbor. Service and worship are linked, likewise, in relationship to each other as well as in relationship to work. Kenneth Kirk distinguishes two very different types of service in the modern world: (1) service of humility and (2) service of patronage. Kirk states that "only the former...has real worth."[83] "Once this is recognized," he continues,

> it becomes not unreasonable to suggest that worship alone guarantees to service that quality of humility without which it is no service at all; and therefore that worship may claim and must be allowed a substantive position in the Christian ideal....So far from being a selfish goal, worship [which includes contemplation and prayer] is the only way to unselfishness which the Christian has at his [or her] command....[A]part from an atmosphere of worship, every act of service avails only to inflate the agent's sense of patronage.[84]

To continue re-connecting disparate "parts" in a movement toward integrality and wholeness, we see the importance of attitude in work. Kirk points out that "disinterested service is the only service that is serviceable; and disinterestedness comes by the life of worship alone."[85]

So we "come round right" once more. Ever caught in the web of means and ends, we must continue on our path(s) toward fulfillment, opening ourselves to the perfection God offers. And the medium as well as the "place" in which we "work out our salvation" is our daily work.

4

THE SOCIO-ETHIC OF

SPIRITUAL WORK

If when we plunge our hand into a bowl of water,
Or stir up the fire with the bellows
Or tabulate interminable columns of figures on our
  book-keeping table,
Or, burnt by the sun, we are plunged in the mud of the
  rice-field,
Or standing by the smelter's furnace
We do not fulfill the same religious life as if in prayer
  in a monastery, the world will never be saved.

M. Gandhi[1]

William Morris' vision and understanding is that of the intimate interweaving of beauty, pleasure, art, leisure, and work. The arts can, will, and do beautify our labor, thus ending dull work and its wearying slavery. Art overcomes the curse of labor by giving us pleasure in our work. But, achieving this state of affairs, i.e., the end of labor's curse, is "...wrapped up...with changes political and social...."[2] Ending dull work and its wearying slavery is connected with the goals of Liberty, Equality, and Fraternity; which when realized will allow for leisure from poverty and its related "sordid cares," and which, along with the arts, bring us to live and to appreciate a "...renewed simplicity of life ...in which we shall have leisure to think about our work...."[3]

Having shown in the previous chapters that there is no demarcation between the secular and the sacred, that, indeed, all of life is sacred and that whatever difference may appear is due simply to ignorance or to a forgetfulness (the two being, in essence, one and the same), it now remains for us to explore the implications this awareness has for the structures and processes of the building of community, the social and economic dimensions of persons and of societies.

I have articulated this exploration in a manner which addresses the over-riding concerns of moral and social ethics. However, as stated in the introductory comments, I am not proposing an ethic of work. The nature of my subject, i.e., work, being what it is, however, it is impossible not to encounter the ethical realm. Besides, designating certain topics "ethical" does not isolate those topics from the mainstream of life. As people course through life, as blood through the body, we contact and intermingle with varied subject matter. Such it is with our abstracted, intellectual concepts: they help us define and articulate the parts of our life but they are just that, parts, and not the whole.

I am proposing that the arena of human work is not separate from our search for meaning and fulfillment. The questions of where and how we work can not be separated from the questions of where and how we worship. Church and workplace must not be viewed through separate lenses. Where ever we are is sacred ground. Every place and every time is a worthy place and time to love God and neighbor; to serve God and neighbor. Service, as seen in light of the Christian monastic tradition[4] and the Hindu way of Karma Yoga, provides *the key* in unraveling apparent contradictions. Service, understood as charity or selfless service, is the key which unlocks the transformative potentials in persons and in society and thus opens the doorway for the building of community.

Building community occurs when the dignity of persons is recognized and is subsequently acted upon through the participation of said persons. This participation, which is the manifestation of the freedom and rationality of the persons—which is their dignity—acts as the dynamic which transforms the bonds of life in society and thus builds community. Work—the (daily) activity of persons—is the arena in which this transformation is enacted. These dyanmic relationships of work are graphically portrayed on page 73. The appropriate attitude in performing one's work is that of service: service to God and service to neighbor. Arriving at this conclusion is not, as we have seen above in chapters one and two, disconnected from one's religious convictions and one's faith. Veritably,

> [t]he faith has got more to do with the job than we
> realized. And the faith "working out" in the job has got

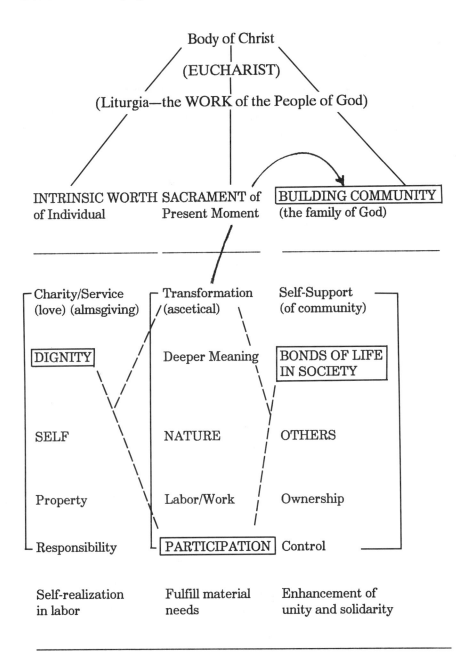

more to do with the set-up of the community than we
realized. It is only when treated as a "cosmos of call-
ings" (Troeltsch, vol.I, p. 293) that the world can ever
know real peace, in which liberty and order shall lie
down together in a responsible society, whose citizens
are free because in their souls and in their work the
hand of God is plain.[5]

THE INTRINSIC WORTH OF EACH PERSON

So God created human beings in God's own image, in
the image of God God created humans; male and
female God created them.

(Genesis 1:27, RSV, inclusive)

"[Humanity] as the Subject of Work": This theme pervades Pope
John Paul II's encyclical *Laborem Exercens*. And it provides a solid
foundation upon which to build a spiritual theology of work. At the
heart is Jesus Christ who "devoted most of the years of his life on
earth to manual work at the carpenter's bench." And this life, the fact
that it was as a worker, is "...in itself the most eloquent 'gospel of
work'."[6]

Already we have diverged from the classical world which degraded
manual labor, considering it antithetical to contemplation and the life
of reason and freedom. A very radical change, because "[w]ork is good
[only] for what the Greek called *banausoi*—the Helots and slaves
—not for the free Hellenes. The Greek free man [the citizen of the
polis] should be exempt from this necessity...."[7] The striving to
become free from necessity, from the biological and physical necessities of survival animated much of classical Greek thought and life.
This struggle to transcend work intensified among the Greeks "...with
the increasing demands of *polis* life upon the time of the citizens and
its insistence on their abstention (*skhole*) from all but political activities, until [by the late fifth century] it covered everything that de-
manded an effort."[8] Henceforth, the amount of effort required
determined the classification of occupations among the Greeks; the
"higher" being those requiring least effort and the "lower" being those
requiring most effort.

Another formulation was devised by the ancient Hindu culture which ranked occupations in a four-tiered social hierarchy. Similar to Hellenistic culture and medieval Europe, topmost are the Brahmans or priests, dealing as they do exclusively with "spiritual" or religious activities. Next down on the ladder are the Kshatriyas, the noble warrior caste which has the duty of government and war. Below them are the merchants, Vaisyas, those involved with commerce. And last, the Shudras, the artisans who make things from the earth's materials, including musicians, cooks, and what we today call skilled tradespeople. Outside and below the caste system itself is the large grouping of those people who perform the so-called menial tasks such as growing food and collecting garbage, the Outcasts or Pariahs. Classifications in this system, originally determined by race, came to be determined by the occupation held, into which a person is born.

What the Greeks of the classical world, the Aryans and Brahmins of ancient India, and others who distinguish classes of people by the kind of work done do not understand is that it is not the work that determines the "status" or "purity" of the person but the person him or her self who determines, as such, his or her status or purity. It is not the material on which a person works, it is not the hours or the place in which a person works, it is not even the use of the finished product or service resulting from the person's work that determines the worth of the person. The sources of the dignity of work are to be sought in the worker, in the person, i.e., in the subject themselves, and not in the kind of work, i.e., in the objective dimension. "Work is for [humanity] not [humanity] for work."[9]

I would like to use the example of collecting garbage to illustrate the possibility of any job being the place of working out one's own salvation through the finding of pleasure in work. Garbage collection will always be a human (community) reality, and thus, people to collect the garbage (garbage collectors) will always be necessary. Someone has got to do it, unless we eliminate garbage; a highly unlikely prospect.

Another way to state this point is that any job necessary to the welfare and social life of a community of persons is work of importance—be it teaching, legislation, or collecting garbage. Therefore, to degrade the job of garbage collector is to degrade the person doing the work, the importance of the work itself, and subsequently, the life of the community.

A qualification: I do not mean to say that the work in question has to be pleasant. The pleasurableness of a particular job is not at issue. What is at issue is the dignity of the worker and the importance of the job itself.

Collecting garbage is not a pleasant job. It is dirty, smelly, and physically taxing. Yet, there are people who choose to be garbage collectors. Granted, some do it for the money (garbage collectors in the city of San Francisco, for instance, were always among the better paid workers in the city), but others are choosing to enter this line of work as a vehicle for social change. These latter people are those working at recycling centers, which are, however one words it, garbage collection centers. That which has changed, that which is different, is the consciousness and understanding of the nature of the substance collected: it is no longer something wasteful and useless, but rather, it is now something of value which can be re-used or re-cycled. With this change of consciousness comes a different attitude among the workers; garbage collectors are now recyclers. They now take pleasure, or at least pride, in their work and tackle it with a new vigor and enthusiasm, solving new problems as they are encountered. There is a feeling of camaraderie with fellow workers.

Granted, a shift in the type of job reality illustrated, i.e., from garbage collector to recycler, demands change in personal and social consciousness as well as in social structures and policies. But it clearly shows that such a change is possible and it points out that even the job of garbage collector is worthy work. This example also illustrates two central elements of a spirituality of work; the attitude of the worker(s), and the understanding of work as service.

> In fact, in the final analysis it is always [humanity] who is the purpose of work, whatever work it is that is done by [humanity]—even if the common scale of values rates it as the merest "service," as the most monotonous, even the most alienating work.[10]

What, then, is Humanity? What is humanity that we should be so concerned about our dignity? What is the significance of the "person"? Why is the person important in discussing work? I shall pursue these questions of anthropology initially for, as Forrester says in *Christian Vocation*, "...we cannot understand what work is meant to be except by realizing what [humanity] is and is meant to be."[11]

The scriptural quotation at the beginning of this section informs us that humanity—men and women at large, but also present or "held" in each man or woman—is created in the image of God. It is that very fact which defines us as persons. John Paul II elaborates on this. He says that a person is "...a subjective being capable of acting in a planned and rational way, capable of deciding about himself [or herself] and with a tendency to self-realization."[12] In other words, it is our free will and rationality which reflects God in each and every person.

That God is imaged in all men and women is of significance. There are not some people who happen to be made in God's image and others who are not so made. All people are God's children. All of us live on this one, small sphere cruising through space. Each woman, man, and child, regardless of race, language, religion, nationality, IQ, or manual dexterity, is the image of God. And God, being the source of all that is—that energy and consciousness which created and sustains all—is for us humans mystery-filled, because God goes beyond description and conceptual grasp. And because God is mystery we know and speak about God and what pertains to God as holy and sacred. Surely, that created by God pertains to God. Each person, therefore, in addition to being a child of God, or more precisely, as a result of being a child of God, is holy and sacred. As a sacred and holy being each person is by nature worthy: by birth; by the fact of being alive.

Of course, people do different things with the gift of life. Some rise to the opportunity while others degenerate and abuse or loose the gift. There are numerous explanations as to why and how this happens—original sin, ignorance, class exploitation—but the debate is beyond the scope and intention of this book. My point is not to deny that there are different qualities and characteristics of people but rather, to express it positively, simply that the gift of life endows a person, any person, with worth and dignity. Each of us takes it from there and does what we will.

"Doing what we will." Here we have two important emphases. First, the act of doing: our work. Second, the act of will: our *free* will. In our doing we collaborate with God in creating. Or, to say it as John Paul II does, we fulfill our (Humanity's) role in subduing the earth and gaining dominion over it, through our work.

M.D.Chenu, O.P., grounds his *Theology of Work* on the basis of an accurate understanding of the relationship between humanity and nature. Chenu chooses the Eastern theologians as his primary source because, "...in contrast to the Fathers of the Latin church, ...the Greeks devoted a great deal of attention to..." this relationship.[13] Indeed, they revived "...one of the great anthropological themes of antiquity, they defined man [humanity] as a 'microcosm'."[14]

The theologian Chenu singles out to illustrate his co-creationist perspective is St. Maximus the Confessor, "...whose vision of the world was the ripe harvest of Greek philosophic, theological and mystical thought."[15] The relationship between Humanity and the Universe is one of co-creation in which humanity participates in its own evolution by finding, exploiting and spiritualizing Nature through work. Indeed, human work ("Homo faber") according to Chenu, "...is rightfully placed in Christian, if not in 'classic' humanism."[16] For work is the human creation by which dominion over nature is accomplished, thus realizing the divine plan, "...even with its possible dangers."[17] Chenu explains that humanity is the "transforming force"[18] through which the cosmos itself enters into "...the whole economy of salvation,"[19] in which all things are reunited in a procession toward their original unity in the One Supreme God.

In our willing we reflect God's characteristic of freedom. God has endowed humans with free will. We are therefore responsible for our actions. *We* are responsible, not something outside us, not someone else. And if responsible for our actions, responsible, too, for their intended consequences. It is as Gregory Baum remarks in his commentary on *Laborem Exercens*, "[Humanity] remains subject, [irregardless of conditions, and thus,] summoned to responsibility."[20] The inherent dignity of persons, which stems from being created in God's image with free will and rationality, underlies the priority of persons over work of any type. Responsibility is an expression of our human dignity.

"...Any genuine respect for human dignity demands that we cultivate and strengthen the bonds of solidarity among us."[21] There is a relationship between peoples that needs to be cultivated and strengthened because it is part of our very nature as humans. We are social beings. You cannot be human by yourself. It requires others; other persons.

As social beings we are members one of another; members of one body: the body of Christ. Each person is worthy and equal before

God. All people are here for a reason. All people are necessary and worthy parts of the whole body and creation.

For what reason, though, are we here? For what purpose, what end, are we here in this body on this earth? For those of the Christian faith I would venture to say that the most fundamental conviction is that "...human life is fulfilled in the knowledge and love of the living God."[22] This goal is not unique to Christianity. It is described variously by the religious traditions of the world as "perfection"—be ye therefore as perfect as your father in heaven is perfect—or as "the kingdom," "salvation," "nirvana," "liberation," "enlightenment," and so forth.[23]

We grow into this knowledge and love of God. We work for it and toward it—it is a goal. And as we strive toward our goal we become the likeness of God, growing from the image of God of which we already partake. As we strive toward our goal we are transformed. This transformation is a restoration of our dignity which occurs in our work. The participation of persons who have recognized their dignity leads, through their participation as workers, to the transformation of the bonds of life in society, and thus is fundamental to the building of community.

This bond, at least within the Christian church, is best exemplified in the eucharist. It is here, at the table, that the multi-hued church (the body of Christ) is brought together in fellowship. The shared bread and wine is the visible embodiment of the bandied-about slogan: unity in diversity. Coming from diverse cultures and walks of life Christians are unified by sharing from the one loaf. By partaking of the body of Christ each Christian, and all of them (us), becomes, in truth, part of that very body. "You are what you eat."

The eucharist is the sharing, actually and symbolically, of the fruits of our labor.

> Every once in a while the mother paused in her eulogy to stir the fire burning in the fireplace, adding a new dry log. Martha, Don Benedetto's sister, came. The peasants of the neighborhood came. Some left their places and departed. The elder Murica, standing at the head of the table, gave food and drink to the men around him.
>
> "It was he," he said, "who helped to sow, to weed,

to thresh, to mill the grain from which this bread was made. Take it and eat it; this is his bread."

Some others arrived. The father gave them something to drink and said, "It was he who helped me to prune, to spray, to weed and to harvest the grapes which went into this wine. Drink; this is his wine."

The men ate and drank. Some of them bathed the bread in the wine.

Some beggars arrived.

"Let them in," said the mother.

"Maybe they've been sent to spy on us," someone murmured.

"Let them in. We'll have to take this risk. Many have given food to Jesus without knowing it in feeding beggars and giving them to drink."

"Eat and drink," said the father.

Finding himself in front of Pietro, the father observed him and asked, "Where are you from?"

"From Orta," he said.

"What's your name?"

Annina came up to the old man and whispered a name into his ear. He looked pleased and embraced Pietro.

"I knew your father when I was young," he told Pietro. "He bought a horse from me at a fair. I heard about you from that son whom I have lost. Sit here between his mother and his bride and have something to drink yourself."

The men around the table were eating and drinking.

"The bread is made from many ears of grain," said Pietro. "Therefore it signifies unity. The wine is made from many grapes, and therefore it, too, signifies unity. A unity of similar things, equal and united. Therefore it means truth and brotherhood, too; these are things which go well together."

"The bread and wine of communion," said an old man. "The grain and the grape which has been trampled upon. The body and the blood."[24]

We bring the fruits of our labor, our gifts of work (money), the fields (bread and wine), and ourselves, and placing them on the common table they are subsequently re-distributed to all who would partake of their life-giving qualities. In this sharing we witness the uplifting power of recognized and accepted human dignity.

From the bounty of our fields we bring the bread and the wine which has been transformed through our work. In this act of bringing we share ourselves with one another. We also share Christ with one another. And Christ shares with us, for the fruits of our labor are—by whatever means one wishes to explain it—Christ's body, and Christ has given his all to us. In partaking of the eucharistic feast we are reminded that we are accepted, as we are, by Christ. Furthermore, through this acceptance we are sure of our human dignity.

This feast is known as "communion." In it and through it we commune: both with all other Christians, gathered as we are at table in fellowship; and also with God through Christ. Thus, we manifest our solidarity with not only Christians but with all others: those who have and do play a part in getting the bread to the table, from the farm to the home and the church.

The apostle Paul, in his first letter to the church at Corinth, provides the most familiar and one of the best models of human solidarity. Paul speaks in the twelfth chapter of his letter about the different persons constituting the different parts of a body—the body of Christ, the church. Each part is different and unique; each part is necessary to the functioning of the whole. The parts are not interchangeable but they are complementary. One cannot say to the other, "I have no need of you" (12:21). This community of solidarity is conveyed in the passage, "If one member suffers, all suffer together; if one member is honored, all rejoice together" (12:26).

All are necessary and worthy for the whole body (church, community, world, work). There is, veritably, a unity in diversity, but only with some unifying factor. In the case of the Christian Church, that unifying factor is Jesus the Christ.

Within the human community of all people both individual persons and the body as a unit seek wholeness and fulfillment. Transformation is sought—at the least, it is desired—by individuals and by society. The dynamic behind transformation, the engaging power which enables transformation, is participation. Participation by individual persons in their journey toward fulfillment is both the vehicle

and the fuel which carries them along; which makes personal transformation possible. The same is true for social transformation. Participation by members of society is crucial. This participation, however,
depends upon the realization and the acceptance, by each person, of
his or her innate dignity.

But people cannot live alone. The nature of humanness is dependent upon human society. We are social beings. Without others,
without living and working with other human beings we cannot survive (literally live), let alone know what it is to be human. We are
dependent one upon another. Individual transformation is therefore
realized within community, in interaction with other persons, in interaction with one's work. As Christianity teaches, it is by giving to and
sharing with others that we truly live, that we have life abundant.
Within the church we share the fruits of our labor visibly, especially in
the eucharist, in the common meal shared at the common table.

Human dignity and social solidarity are fundamental to God's
purpose, and hence the make-up of our world. When denied, God's
will is thwarted, and, at the least, the biblical vision and mandate is
obstructed.

Inherent in the nature of human dignity is the implacable realization that persons are ends and not means. Persons, both individually
and in community, hold within themselves the purpose and function
and meaning of life. All systems human-made (economic, political,
religious, technological) are thus judged upon their treatment of
persons. Is this system, item, or policy detrimental to persons or is it
conducive to personhood; to the growth and development of the
persons affected? Another watch-word here is that these should be
transformational rather than therapeutic. Adjusting a person to a bad
system, policy or lifestyle is not conducive to personhood and growth.

As I have mentioned, this transformation and fulfillment leads to
the knowledge and love of God. This state of being has been called by
such names as holiness, beatitude, and sanctification. It is the goal
stated by ascetics, mystics, and saints of all religious and many philosophical traditions. It is not an unusual nor a strange goal to humankind, though it seems to have been out of favor these last few hun-
dred years in that one part of the world called "the West."

The major religious traditions claim this goal for all people and
not only for an elite. Christ calls all men and women to him. Buddha,
in his compassion, remains in the world until all sentient beings are

saved. All people are called to know and love God. To realize this knowledge and state of being is the vocation of every woman and man.

Holiness is addressed to every person in every walk of life. Sanctity is the vocation of every person and it is, of necessity, achieved in the midst of the world. Clement of Alexandria states:

> ...Practice husbandry, we say, if you are a husbandman; but while you till your fields, know God. Sail the sea, you who are devoted to navigation, yet call the whilst on the heavenly Pilot....[25]

Early in his book, *Christian Vocation: Studies in Faith and Work*, W. R. Forrester states the same position as Clement. Forrester remarks that our task, as Christians today, is "...to lead men [and women] to make their choices and do their daily work, be they parsons or scavengers, with a sense of vocation and so to 'work out their own salvation'."[26] He continues, "If we are to be able to redeem men [and women] in our age of techniques and depersonalizing machinery, we must be able to make real to them the great truths of Creation, Providence and Grace, as these are personalized in the doctrine of vocation."[27] It is my contention that the knowledge and experience of these "great truths" can only be made real through the spiritual path, i.e., through pursuing the life of perfection in the midst of daily life.

Our present situation calls for a synthesis of the many strands of Christian experience and acquired wisdom wrought in the search for wisdom (philosophy) and beauty (philokalia) over the last 2000 years. Drawing from the monastic traditions of East and West (Orthodox and Roman Catholic) and from Reformation and later Protestants, I propose a practical spirituality which would reap the fruit of all traditions. The monastic traditions provide a wealth of tried-and-true practices or rules for pilgrims on the path toward perfection. As I see it, the Protestant Reformation threw out "the baby with the bath water." In cleaning house the reformers discarded important and necessary disciplines and attitudes (i.e., metaphysical understandings and perspectives), such as charity, contemplation, striving for detachment from worldly goods (and idols). At the time these had, so it would seem, degenerated and become distorted and were misunderstood and therefore relegated to the scrap heap of "by-gone eras" and "superstitions."

Protestants did, however, hit upon a true gem. Luther, Calvin, and later Wesley, talked about achieving perfection *in* the world, in the daily pursuits of women and men. The way was, once again, opened to everyone *where they were.* The secluded monastery was not the only place where God was found or where a person could seek God. Men and women of all walks of life could seek and find spiritual fulfillment in the home, the field, the shop, the factory. Lost, however, in this (re)discovery were the means by which to accomplish the task. Lost was the requisite disposition of detachment and contemplation as the central guiding font of action and work. Lost, despite Bunyon's efforts, was the understanding that we are but pilgrims on this earth —with a destination far different (in kind and quantity) than the accumulation of wealth and power. Lost was the proper relationship between the end and the means of human life. Growing toward perfection came to be judged by growing abundance and material possessions rather than growing in grace and inner transformation. And this, the awareness of the possibility of inner transformation, was the greatest loss of all. For without the possibility of such a transformation—of real, concrete stages or levels of spiritual growth and development—there is no point to ascetic practices. What indeed would be the point of striving for detachment (such a state would never contribute to the accumulation of wealth) in a world devoid of any thing beyond the mind or the senses.

Essential to our contemporary situation is the blending of these traditions. We need to work for perfection, to strive for spiritual fulfillment, in the midst of our daily pursuits, as Protestants have taught. Yet, we need to do so in the light of and with the help and application of the many spiritual practices and metaphysical understandings of the monastic and theological traditions of the Orthodox and Roman Catholic traditions. Of course, the same inclusiveness is also applicable to all religious traditions.

SACRAMENT OF THE PRESENT MOMENT

"In the beginning God created...(all things)...and saw that it was very good." (Genesis 1:1–31) "And it was good" means all of it. All the parts and pieces and animals, and heavens and waters and stars, and men and women, all were part and parcel of "it." It was not "it" without the whole package. God did not say it was good after the first day, nor the fourth, nor the fifth day, but only after the whole creation was complete. Its being whole and complete helped make it good. All of creation is of and by God, the Creator. All of creation is therefore sacred; it carries a sacramental quality by its very nature.

Yet there is a forgetfulness of the sacramental nature of all of creation. We humans have difficulty accepting death, storms, or poisonous snakes as "good."[28]

We forget that all of creation is sacred when we divide life into opposing camps such as "religious" and "political" or "spiritual" and "material." Forgetfulness of creation's sacramental nature is reflected in efforts to deny the sacred or ethics a place in partial realms like economics, science, international relations, energy production, or the workplace.

Another example of our human forgetfulness appears in our personality theories which advocate satisfying all of one's desires and urges as the means to overcome and transcend them; as though adding fuel to a fire will somehow extinguish it. This sense of our being only our senses, or of our being only influenced by the physically observable realm results from our forgetfulness of the sacredness, and therefore oneness, of *all* of creation. The idea that we only are born, live, and die with nothing more to life—either before and/or after, or more meaningful—is a consequence of our forgetfulness of the multi-faceted construction (the creativeness) of God's creation.

The separation of life into the various categories and compartments of modern life—work, school, vacation, hobbies, art, church, house-work, rest—are real but their distortion derives from the fact that they are sociologically derived classifications designed to help study and clarify the distinct parts of human life. In the process they have lost their tether and now float about listlessly in disarray. The forest has been lost in the analysis of the trees.

Our task today, as workers, as Christians, as religious people, as human beings, is to set about on a journey of re-discovering the entire forest with the knowledge and insight garnered from our analysis of some of the separate trees—by no means all of them; actually we could say we have really only explored one glen on one hillside of the forest. We are finding many of the old-timers, the forest guides, and asking their help. That is a good sign. They remind us of creation's sacramental nature, of the oneness of creation, of the path to wholeness.

One of the many things these old forest guides tell us is that all means of livelihood are potential ways toward spiritual fulfillment.[29] Applying this understanding to our current situation and the world of work we must admit that all types and places of work are possible ways and places for the journey toward wholeness. As such, all types and places of work are sacred. The workplace is sacred ground for what occurs there is a part of creation.

Most people do not perceive of the workplace as a sacred place because of our forgetfulness. We do not think of the workplace sacramentally because we do not allow for the possibility of realizing spiritual fulfillment in our daily lives; in the midst of our daily work. In this regard our attitude is pivotal. The thoughts we hold in our minds determine the perceptions we have of what, or can, take(s) place in and with our work.[30]

Our thoughts determine who and what we are and what we perceive. If our thoughts change, who and what we are and what we perceive will change. As a worker, if my thoughts undergo a change regarding the nature of my work and the place in which I work, such that I come to perceive my work as a means for my personal growth and transformation, and my place of work as sacred ground, then my attitude toward both my work and my workplace (not to mention my fellow workers) will undergo a profound transformation.[31]

We return to the centrality of understanding the proper relationship between means and ends. Work seen merely as an end in itself, as simply the production of some thing or service, paves the way for alienation; the consequences of which are people thinking of and experiencing work as something separate from themselves, separate from the significant parts of their lives. If work is just an added burden to life that out of necessity we are forced to undertake, it is no wonder men and women count the minutes to closing time. No one in their right mind chooses degrading and demeaning work. That is why such work in the classical world was performed by slaves.

Work viewed, on the other hand, as a *means* to an end, beyond the work and/or its product or service, can be tolerated at worst, or ennobling and enlightening at best. Without a proper understanding of the relationship between means and ends I do not see how contemporary people will ever transcend the alienating potential of work.

It is just as important to pay attention to the means of work as it is to its end. Indeed, "...all the secret of success..." lies in this awareness, Swami Vivekananda tells us in *Work and its Secret*. Cutting through the proliferating verbiage on this subject, Vivekananda states simply the proper relationship:

> With the means all right, the end must come. We forget that it is the cause that produces the effect. ...The means are the cause; attention to the means, therefore, is the great secret of life.[32]

Our attention to the means of work, i.e., both the modes of production and the attitude of each worker, will provide the pivot upon which to turn (*metanoia*) our perceived reality of the secular nature of work round right to our viewing work in its profoundly sacramental reality.

This is not squabbling over some refined esoteric point. This *is* the point of conversion. This is the heart of the whole matter.

Everywhere and at all times is the place for spiritual endeavors, including the workplace. All is holy. All is sacred. All is sacralized because there is no place or time where God is not. And where God is, that place and time is sacred ground.

BUILDING COMMUNITY: "THE GREAT WORKBENCH"

Community occurs when the dignity of persons is recognized and is subsequently acted upon through the participation of said persons. This participation, which is the manifestation of the freedom and rationality of the persons—which is their dignity—acts as the dynamic which transforms the bonds of life in society and thus builds community. Work, the daily activity of people, is the arena in which this transformation is enacted.

> To say that [humanity] is a social and political animal is tantamount to saying that men [and women] are shaped by the forms of their sociability, and I cannot think of any more direct way to a better understanding

of men [and women] and of what society can do for
men [and women] than through the study of these
forms.[33]

While I cannot pursue an in-depth sociological or philosophical
inquiry of all "these forms" of human sociability I do propose to highlight three aspects of human relationships important to any practical
spirituality: our relationships with other people; with nature; and with
our own self/selves.

The three poles of relationship (self, nature, others) intersect the
three central triads of my argument: Intrinsic Worth of the Individual;
Sacrament of the Moment; and Building Community (see graph on
page 73). The relationship triad links the three central triads through
the different dimensions of relationships. Here we have another loop
within larger circles in the construction of the body of Christ. And so,
while addressing the topic of "building community" we are also directly connected to the topics of the intrinsic worth of the individual and
the sacrament of the present moment. And thus, while I attempt to
distinguish these categories in separate chapters, the very nature of
their unity fights the academic propensity for separation.

The three dimensions of relationship I have chosen to work with
are, obviously, from Karl Marx's analysis and observation, wherein the
subject, i.e., the person, has become alienated (in Marx's analysis
through the divisive characteristics of the means of production of
monopoly, industrial capitalism) from their fellow workers (others),
from the work itself (nature), and indeed, from one's own self.

Relationship with One's Self

Healthy, wholesome relationships with ourselves, each person
with their own being, are grounded on the solid rock of self respect
and dignity. Made as we are in the image of God, an inherent human
attribute is dignity. We are, each of us, born of noble blood.

The very cornerstone of human architecture is freedom of the
will. Having free will human beings are therefore responsible for their
intentions and actions. But our economic and social system has gone
about destroying and denying this central human attribute.

We are made of a whole but our life leads to disintegration; to separation and alienation from ourselves, from our wholeness.

> In what does the alienation of labor consist? First, that the work is external to the worker, that it is not a part of his [or her] nature, that consequently he [or she] does not fulfill himself [or herself] in his [or her] work but denies himself [or herself], has a feeling of misery, not of well-being....The worker therefore feels himself [or herself] at home only during his [or her] leisure, whereas at work he [or she] feels homeless.[34]

"Labor is both eminently personal and eminently social."[35] In its personal aspect labor's impact on people is central and profound. As Gregory Baum states, "...the most important aspect of [humanity] laboring is precisely his [and her] personal transformation as subject...."[36]

I am in general agreement with Baum, as well as with Pope John Paul II and others of a personalist persuasion; especially with regard to this issue of work and the well-being of the individual worker(s). For the application of the personalist principle widens Marxist notions *a la* socialism and the process of social transformation.[37] But, "Both art and craft must take part in any activity which has the power to transform."[38]

It will not do merely to work if a person would be transformed. There must be a self-imposed intentionality about one's work if it would be called "art" and/or "craft", thereby giving the potential (it is not a guarantee) of personal transformation.[39] On this point I am in agreement with D.M. Dooling and the other authors of *A Way of Working*. In other words, if art and craft are absent from work there is very little possibility of the "workers" becoming transformed; at least within the performance of their work. This is the case for so many workers today, that there is no art or craft involved in their work. Yet, precisely the recovery of such a reality is the key for overcoming the alienation from themselves that workers experience.

The recovery of the attitude of art and craft within our daily work does not necessarily imply the termination of the tension between physical toil or "rough labor" and creative expression. Such a recovery does, however, allow the possibility of establishing a relationship with one's self *through* the marriage of these counterpoising forces. Indeed, it is within this marriage that humanity comes to know itself. It is within this tension of opposites that men and women struggle to become truly human.

> For the crafts[person], as well as the alchemist, [and I would include the worker] knows that his [or her] central task is the creation of himself [or herself]; and it is above all for this aim that he [or she] strives with endless patience, separating "the subtle from the gross, softly and with great care," to make what his [or her] hands touch turn to gold.[40]

It is in the struggling with this ever-present paradox that persons forge a transformation of themselves.

The tension between work and labor, between toil and creation, is real. What is false is the notion that there is no connection and that the tension cannot be transcended.

We establish a relationship with our selves through a relationship to our work. This in turn incorporates a voluntary intentionality which in turn enables a commitment to responsibility. And this commitment to responsibility, emerging as it does from an awareness of one's inherent dignity, enables one to strive for quality which, of course, is intertwined with art and craft. Because of the intentionality, i.e., purpose and meaning, invested in one's work the struggle with and in one's work is the means by which one's personal transformation is wrought. Thus it is that work enables us to establish a relationship with our self, and also with nature and with others.

Relationship with Other People

> What the world needs is the statement of a new faith in which community will replace property as the sacrament of life.[41]

> ..."holding   all   things   in   common"(Acts   2:44–45;

4:32–37), suggests not only shared material possessions but, even more basically, a spirit of friendship
and mutual concern among all its members.[42]

Christians have one great resource: they can call Fraternity to their aid, for this one of the great three
[Liberty, Equality, Fraternity] is really nearer than
either of her sisters to the divine heart.[43]

Social interaction is to reflect the norms of the cove-
nant: reciprocal responsibility, mercy and truthfulness.
Living like this brings "wholeness" (Shalom).[44]

The prophets and Jesus stood for the weak. It was
their wisdom that the common welfare was to be
found by organizing society to meet the needs and
develop the lives of the people at the bottom. In that
way fellowship and capacity were to increase....This
type of morality...works for unity. It is the vital core of
a creative religion.[45]

Communal solidarity is at the heart of the biblical
understanding of the human condition.[46]

The U.S. Roman Catholic Bishops' Pastoral on the Economy
continues from this last quotation to show "...the inseparability of
personal dignity and social solidarity."[47] Indeed, "...men and women
cannot grow to full self-realization in isolation."[48] The qualities of
community, of communal solidarity, make possible this realization in
an atmosphere of "...interaction, interdependence, communication,
collaboration, and—in the fullest form—communion and love."[49]
    The Christian, veritably, all people, stands in the presence of God
not as an individual but "...as a person who exists in loving inter-
personal communion with fellow human beings and therefore with
God...."[50] The relationships of this communal existence are illustrated with the triad:

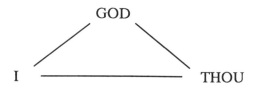

Grounded in scripture and finding expression throughout Christian history, this inner dynamic of "wholeness" (shalom) challenges the person of faith toward an intentional life of "communal solidarity."

> My movement in love towards my fellow-human
> "Thou" is in fact possible because God has taken the
> initial movement in love towards me, a movement to
> which I can only respond via my neighbor (Matthew
> 5:23f.).[51]

As the above triad illustrates there is both a *horizontal* dimension and a *vertical* dimension to life; to the relational dynamic of human, and therefore communal life. The horizontal dimension is our interactions with fellow humans and our relationship with God is the vertical dimension. Moreover, we see from Matthew 5:23f., and this is of capital importance, that the vertical is the main dimension.[52]

Our human want is to separate these two dimensions. By doing so, however, we deprive ourselves of both sustenance and guidance in the form of the vertical, as well as points of reference and nurture in the form of the horizontal. In separating the two dimensions of our lives we literally split ourselves asunder from the source and means of life. It is essential to hold the vertical and the horizontal together if we would be, literally, whole; if we would experience and bring to fruition shalom.

The tendency to divide our poles of existence smacks of a dualism, a heresy Christians have always battled, whose only outcome can be a non-"societied," non-cultured conglomeration of individuals—isolated by their very nature: individual—at odds with one another; and at odds with the source and means of life itself. In the vertical dimension this source and means of life is God, or spirit, and in the horizontal dimension it is human love and affection and, physically, food.[53]

According to theologian Dorothy Sölle, the separation between the horizontal and the vertical is a result of bourgeois consciousness and theology, among other reasons. The Bible, however, does not separate them, states Sölle, "...in terms of a dualism between religion and politics, between the love of God and love for one's neighbor, between religious conduct and human conduct." On the contrary, Sölle continues, "the tendency of Jesus is firmly to hold on to the unity of these two lines of conduct....[L]ife does not consist in two parallel paths, but essentially in their meeting and in their intersection."[54] The debilitating consequence from the "overspecialization of all the particular domains of life,"[55] is our paralysis, our inability to act. Furthermore, accepting such a distinction is "...the most subtle form of atheism,"[56] for it denies the Christian understanding of *one* world which belongs entirely to the Kingdom of God.

Two important implications emerge from this multi-dimensional perspective. First, in that the horizontal and the vertical are not opposed one to the other but rather complement and fulfill each other, they are not separate but one. All is subsumed under the initiative of the divine. The vertical, as such, incorporates the horizontal or, in other words, as I have stated the case above, all is sacred. It is all one: reality, life, the *universe*.

The second implication is precisely that of my title: heaven is here, present in the mundane, earthly dimension of us humans and the soil from which we grow our sustenance. The authors of *An Orthodox Approach to Diaconia* state it a bit differently than I: "...bringing the heavenly into the earthly....But at the same time...the elevation of the earthly into the heavenly places, the fulfillment of every immanent creaturely *telos* (goal) and its transfiguration by grace."[57] The necessity of maintaining both dimensions is the acceptance of the necessity of the divine interpenetrating the human, and vise versa. Thereby, our relationships with other people are grounded in, and thoroughly interpenetrated by divinity—if we allow them to be.

Personal relationships understood within the scope of the vertical dimension call forth qualities exemplified in the biblical scriptures, such as co-operation, responsibility, caring, and humility. These same qualities find articulate expression in other religious traditions as well. In fact, the best commentary I have found on them as they relate to personal relationships and the world of work is by a Tibetan Buddhist. The comments that follow were gleaned from a reading of Tarthang Tulku's gem of a book, *Skillful Means*.[58]

"Without cooperation to bring us together, our work and our relationships suffer, and we lose sight of the delights and benefits of
working closely with each other."[59] Three essential elements of
cooperation are looking outward, opening, and especially caring. We
need to open ourselves—to our bodies, our minds, our senses, and our
feelings. In the process of opening ourselves we are better able to be
open *to* others and *for* others. "Caring and cooperation reveal to us
the many pleasures of work, and the time we spend at work becomes a
source of stimulation and enjoyment....Distinctions between work
and spare time diminish as work is integrated into a harmonious approach to living."[60]

> Work gives us the opportunity to educate our-
> selves, to incorporate higher values into our daily ex-
> periences. By caring for our work, responding fully to
> it, we can begin to understand the nature of our re-
> sponsibility as human beings. For we have a responsi-
> bility to work, to exercise our talents and abilities, to
> contribute our energy to life. Our nature is creative,
> and by expressing it, we constantly generate more
> enthusiasm and creativity, stimulating an ongoing pro-
> cess of enjoyment in the world around us. Working
> willingly, with our full energy and enthusiasm, is our
> way of contributing to life.

> Every kind of work can be a pleasure....As we
> respond with caring and vision to all work, we develop
> our capacity to respond fully to all of life. Every action
> generates positive energy which can be shared with
> others. These qualities of caring and responsiveness
> are the greatest gifts we have to offer.[61]

Responsibility and caring are intimately related. "If we are to act
with responsibility, we need to strengthen our feeling of caring."[62]
And caring, as Talku uses it, is the same as service, as I use it. Indeed,
we are not only responsible for our actions and our work; "As we grow
to understand the nature of existence, we see that *ultimately it is the
truth for which we are responsible.* Though sometimes a lonely position
on which to stand, it is the truth that will liberate us from selfishness,

resentment, fear, and anxiety."[63]

Last, but not least, of the four qualities called forth from God's people in our relationships with other people is that of humility. "Humility is an experience of the commonality of all human beings."[64] In developing a humble attitude our selfish tendencies are transformed into generosity. In generosity we cooperate with and care for others, thus taking responsibility for our lives together on this planet in this life.

Relationship with Nature

> One looks in vain within classical Protestantism's rig-
> oristic sense of vocation for the workman's joy and
> deep satisfaction both in the skill that has enabled him
> [or her] to complete his [or her] task or in the sense of
> having been a kind of obstetrician to set nature free.
> Equally wanting is the Franciscan note of the *Canticle
> to the Sun* where water and earth and even death are
> hailed as sister and brother....[65]

Indeed, humanity has the need

> to manifest (within [humanity's] relation with nature
> and creation) our own redemption in work, in the re-
> demption of the created order.[66]

Generally speaking, Christianity has been rather opposed to a stance of oneness with our brothers and sisters of creation, i.e., the birds and animals; and also the rivers and fields and mountains. This is largely the consequence of a God entirely transcendent; of a God entirely "other."

A mitigating factor against this tendency, both within and outside of Christianity, is the reflections by women on their experiences of human relatedness to nature; on the intermingling of the human and the divine in nature. Among others, contemporary women reflecting on this issue are Rosemary R. Ruether, Letty Russell, and an inter-racial group of seven women who call themselves the Mud Flower Collective.[67] Such reflection is, however, by no means a recent phenomenon only. Two representative women from pre-reformation Europe are the English mystic Julian of Norwich (c.1342–c.1413), and, from the Rhineland, St. Hildegard of Bingen (1098–1179).[68]

Women have traditionally been understood as being in closer touch with nature than the male half of the human race. This understanding rests, largely, on women's monthly, and thereby lunar, menstrual cycle. Even more so, it rests on the fact that they give human birth: it is in the woman and as part of the woman that new human life grows. And women experience first hand the joys and pains of birth itself in their "labor."

Although the conception or creation of new life is a joint act between male and female, women still carry the brunt of child rearing. The nurturing and maintaining of children as they grow from fragile infants into their own persons has been traditionally, and still continues very much to be, the work and responsibility of women. Despite the often unfairness to or exploitation of women exhibited in child rearing, such work would seem to have allowed women, some consciously and others, no doubt, unconsciously, to remain more attuned to the ways of nature than their male counterparts. The processes of giving life and of growth and change so intimately intertwined with the natural world to which we humans belong seem closer to the surface, to consciousness, in women as a result of bearing and raising children.

Whether or not the raising[69] of children remains primarily in the hands of women or becomes more a joint responsibility of women and men, the fact remains that the work of raising children brings one closer to the natural rhythms of growth and change. Furthermore, such activity is truly work, and must therefore be appropriately recognized and respected.

A spirituality that combines art, work, and worship must be intimately tied to Mother Earth. The understanding that all of life is sacred presupposes that all of creation is a unity, a whole, a family. Physical matter is, we now know, actually a contracted bundle of energy. It *is* all one.

> The craft[person]'s struggle with nature is a "kindly struggle" which entails "both the building-up and the wearing-away of their lives."[70]

Furthermore, "All true crafts[persons] are born [to this struggle]...."[71]

The endeavor to overcome or heal the split between prayer and work, contemplation and action, and inner and outer is directly related to healing the split between humankind and nature. To think that "mastery" of the earth implies raping our mother (the very source and support of our being and our existence) and of killing our sisters and brothers (our fellow creatures) is the ultimate of insanity. Or, to be kind, it is the ultimate of mis-directed intentions and a lack of understanding.

It is in and with our everyday lives, or nowhere, that we are going to find our spiritual fulfillment. It is only here—which is everywhere; which is *in* "nature"—that we will realize our being and purpose. The artisan's struggle with nature illustrates the tension inherent in human striving for knowledge and happiness. It is the alchemical struggle between the masculine/solar and the feminine/lunar qualities within each person which must seek a harmony.[72] This striving for harmony is the striving for beauty as exemplified in the artisan. In the mundane work-a-day world this beauty is possible only through art (*a la* William Morris et al.). The danger of modern, industrial (and post-industrial) civilization is that we shall be deprived of the beauty of life through our mis-directed efforts to provide everyone with the so-called luxuries of life through mass-produced consumer goods. That which is misdirected in such an effort is the underlying assumption that beauty is not a necessary ingredient in the products produced for mass consumption. This assumption belies the inherent necessity of beauty, and hence art, to a complete and harmonious life. As William Morris says,

> ...for that beauty, which is what is meant by *art*, ... is, I contend, no mere accident to human life, which people can take or leave as they choose, but a positive necessity of life, if we are to live as nature meant us to; that is, unless we are content to be less than men [and women].[73]

When relating this idea of beauty to our relationships with nature it becomes an affair of morality as well as of strictly art. For art cannot be dissociated from morality, politics, and religion. "Truth in these great matters of principle is one, and it is only in formal treatises that it can be split up diversely...."[74]

Applying Morris' perspective to the social and economic realm, immediately and graphically the far-reaching implications and consequences of such a unified viewpoint become apparent. Morris, ahead of his time in reflecting on ecological matters, pens in his essay "The Beauty of Life," a biting condemnation of "so-called manufacturers" who befoul the air, the land, and the waters:

> ...how can you care about the image of the landscape when you show by your deeds that you don't care for the landscape itself? or what right have you to shut yourself up with beautiful form and colour when you make it impossible for other people to have any share in these things?[75]

> Pray do not forget, that any one who cuts down a tree wantonly or carelessly, especially in a great town or its suburbs, need make no pretense of caring about art.[76]

There is a connection between the artisan and nature, and between the worker and his or her work. The question is: What is this connection? Two triads which "hold" this connection, which "get at" the relationship inherent in a person's making and doing are the following:

Yet beauty in and of itself is not enough to transform the lives of workers. More is required than merely gardens or a beautiful building, for instance. "Good conditions of work can be only realized naturally and without affectation by the work which is to be done...being in all ways reasonable and fit for human beings."[77]

EPILOGUE

Pervading as it does, all of life, the temptation in addressing the issue of work is to include everything. The struggle in writing this book has been to restrict the bounds of discussion to the fields of art, worship, spirituality, and, to a very limited extent, economic and social theory, as they impinge upon work. Within the all-pervasive realm of work I have attempted to focus specifically on how persons are to find spiritual fulfillment in everyday (work) life.

Initially, my thoughts on work dealt with the social and economic aspects; I had thought to write a theology of work or a new ethic of work. However, I was also, at the time, dealing with the issue of spirituality; asking questions like, "How do we/I make spirituality applicable today?," "What are the similarities between Christian spirituality and the spiritualities of other religious traditions?," "Does spirituality have anything to say to our economic and social life?" My need to forge a union of these two interests found expression in this project, the writing of which has been for me part of my personal spiritual quest. It has been a vehicle for integrating the personal and the social, and also, Christianity and other traditions.

My search has led me to the conclusion, in agreement with Robert Bellah and Pope John Paul II, for instance, that work is at the heart of the social question. As Bellah states it in his testimony before the committee of the National Conference of Catholic Bishops drafting their pastoral letter "Catholic Social Teaching and the U.S. Economy,"

> ...economic planning and policy in our society must think above all about the nature of work and the pattern of jobs, for everything else depends on that.

> Since work is the point of intersection between the human person and an economic system, it seems to me the strategic point of entry for ethical reflection and Christian witness...we need to recover a sense of

work as "sharing in the activity of the creator."[1]

I address the socio-economic aspects of a spirituality of work, but I focus on the more personal aspects of spiritual fulfillment related to work because I understand the human person to be central. Although a simultaneous treatment is necessary for a complete healing, the alienation of the individual person from him or her self is the lynch-pin in addressing any other types of alienation, such as that from others and/or that from nature. People must be (re-)made whole: the person and God, all of one piece, as Eric Gill says; we must re-establish the "integrality" of the person, of life.

The challenge, therefore, the task before us,

> ...is to live in such a way that there is no duality, no separation between the spiritual path and its manifestation in everyday life. The real challenge is, so to speak, to bring heaven down to earth, where we all live. It is a question of..."applied spirituality."[2]

Ananda Coomaraswamy, in quoting Albert Schweitzer, states, "...'the modern man [or woman] has no longer any spiritual self-confidence at all,' scepticism has gained ascendancy over belief. We no longer trust ourselves but now take our truths and convictions from the associations that have rights over [us]...." This lack of spiritual self-confidence is part of what I am addressing. It is one reason why a spirituality of work is so important: to get people back in touch with themselves, with the power and possibilities inherent in them and in their work.

We spend our lives working. Surely we have a sense (surely we *know*) about how things work; how they should be (how they are). But we no longer listen to ourselves—to that sure small voice within. We no longer trust ourselves, thinking, rather, that "experts" know what is what. And thus, we have abdicated—given up—our very souls, and our freedom.

If we cannot regain a sense of self-knowledge at work, where we spend most of our lives, what hope is there? Must we journey through life in a schizoid maze; feeling we know but never allowed to acknowledge or to manifest our knowledge.

Responsibility seems to be a central factor; but responsibility in a larger context than merely for the immediate product of one's hands. Rather, responsibility as a member of society and as a member of God's family. Indeed, it is *theologically* imperative that the ownership of the means of production reside in the hands of working people in order for them to become responsible men and women; in order for them to realize their true potential and be all that God would have them be.

Alienating work stands condemned for being what it is, alienating. Arguments based on "efficiency," "profitability," or other premises not condemning the de-humanization of the persons affected, are ideological rationalizations. As such, they must be de-mythologized or de-sacralized in order to liberate those held captive to this or that particular illusion.

What human beings have designed and implemented—such as legal and economic statutes and relationships—human beings can re-design and re-implement. In other words, we can change laws, we can change social structures and systems. Since people have created and constructed the structures which hold our thinking and our production, those very structures can be modified or replaced, and new structures created and built in their stead.

The future is not a closed-system. God's power—be it the Holy Spirit, Shakti, or Chi—is limitless. If we listen to and respond to the Gospel mandate "to love justice, seek mercy, and to walk humbly with our God," we can no longer be a party to the de-humanizing economic systems prevalent today throughout most of the world. Whether that system is state capitalism or "free enterprise" capitalism, it is a system which feeds on people, on the soul and blood of men and women, depriving them of their dreams, and of their possibilities for realizing their God-given potential of supreme happiness or beatitude.

People must be (re)made whole: the person and God, all of one piece. We must re-establish the "integrality" of the person, of life. And this must include the social, economic, and political dimensions as well as the individual and inter-personal dimensions. Yet, to preach the Christian doctrine of responsibility to people who, by the nature and condition of their work, can have none is like expecting a sterile person to conceive a child.

> You cannot have responsible human beings in their
> leisure time, if they are not responsible in

> their working time.
> For working is the means of living, and it is life for
>   which we have responsibility.
> You cannot have responsibility for your work unless
>   you have control over it.
> You cannot have control over it unless individually or
>   collectively you own it.
> We have destroyed the ownership and control, and
>   therefore the responsibility of the workers....[3]

What then must we do? Douglas Steere's suggestions of the early 1950's are as applicable today as they were then. We must restore to workers a sense of responsibility for what they are about and we must recover a frame of meaning that [will] give a dimension to work which has almost sunk from view today.[4]

The remedy lies in the sphere of ownership. And by ownership it must be made clear that I am not talking about the ownership of stock or a share in the profits. For under such patronage—the workers remaining only minority "owners"—it is inevitable that production will continue for the sake of profit because good quality is all right,only *if it pays*. It is necessary to reverse the historical process from financial ownership and control of production to the ownership and control by those who do the work rather than the selling. In other words, the ownership of the means of production must belong to the workers. "At present it belongs to the banks and so we have only what *pays* and not what is *good*."[5]

But this sounds like communism, some may say. And I, like Gill, respond, "what of it?" Pope Leo XIII said: "As many as possible of the people should be induced to become owners." Leo XIII further stated in *Rerum Novarum*, "How must one's possessions be used? Man[sic] should not consider his material possessions as his own but as common to all, so as to share them without hesitation when others are in need."

Indeed, if object of human life is sanctification, "labour being the means of life is the appointed means to holiness and thus to beatitude...." And furthermore, "of all kinds of ownership, that of the means of production is the most important, and so important is it that, as Pope Leo XIII says, it is a natural right...it is God's will for man [and woman]."[6]

In order to find fulfillment in life it is *theologically* imperative that working men and women own the means of production.

How, then, are working people to gain ownership? It is not within the scope of this book to present a plan of action. Assuming ownership, however, a few comments are in order to highlight the possibilities of human fulfillment. First, the workers must secure control, then they will be in a position to decide what they want to do. That is to say, then there will be the possibility of change; then both the means and the mode of production will be open questions. The worker-owners can then decide whether they even want to continue with the same routine at all. The factories cannot be closed until and unless the workers are in a position to decide.

Even if workers decide to continue with the factory system at least it will be theirs! The product will be the fruit of their actions and decisions. They will reap the profit—they will make/earn the money directly from their work—no "boss" or outside person(s) being in a position to exploit them. Their ownership will allow them to participate, to be responsible. And in this the possibility is greatly enhanced for their human fulfillment, both individually and socially.

Furthermore, the way is then open for the insertion of the element of *quality*—that subversive notion in a system based on profit and capital. People may then find a way to produce goods for *use*. And in this we come round to the fundamental nature and role of *art*; of the artist in everyone!

The outlook I am suggesting calls for a different, but by no means new, perspective on life than is presently pervasive. In order for workers to view themselves as craftspersons and as artists it is necessary for them, and for all of us, to have a different understanding of who and what we are, which in turn requires a different understanding of the purpose of work and of life. It is not possible to view work as worship unless one views it first as service; and how to understand it as service without first having at least a basic religious or spiritual outlook on life.

So I am calling for a change of outlook, a change of priorities, a change of the basis of our society. It starts with each person, and in this sense it calls for individual responsibility and initiative. It also starts with the church (with any and all religious groups), and with groups of workers, artists, and craftspeople, thus calling forth community responsibility and initiative.

I am calling for a return to the understanding that all of life is sacred, that there is, by the very nature of the case, no such thing as the secular. I am saying that all of life needs to be sacralized and seen as service and as worship.

Today people in America, and in the world at large, are again in need of remembering the intrinsic worth of each and every individual and also of each occupation at which men and women work, especially those involving physical labor.

Walt Whitman invokes this spirit of reverence for the individual person and his or her occupation in his poem "A Song for Occupations."

> A song for occupations!
> In the labor of engines and trades and the labor of
>   fields I find the developments,
> And find the eternal meanings.
>
> Workmen and Workwomen!
> ....
> Why what have you thought of yourself?
> Is it you then that thought yourself less?
> Is it you that thought the President greater than you?
> Or the rich better off than you? or the educated wiser
>   than you?
> (Because you are greasy or pimpled, or were once
>   drunk, or a thief,
> Or that you are dises'd, or rheumatic, or a prostitute,
> Or from frivolity or impotence, or that you are no
>   scholar and never saw your name in print,
> Do you give in that you are any less immortal?)
>
> Souls of men and women! it is not you I call unseen,
>   unheard, untouchable and untouching,
> It is not you I go argue pro and con about, and to
>   settle whether you are alive or no,
> I own publicly who you are, if nobody else owns.
> ....
> I bring what you much need yet always have,
> Not money, amours, dress, eating, erudition, but as

good,
I send no agent or medium, offer no representative of
value, but offer the value itself.
....
The sum of all known reverence I add up in you
whoever you are,
The President is there in the White House for you, it
is not you who are here for him,
The Secretaries act in their bureaus for you, not you
here for them,
The Congress convenes every Twelfth-month for you,
Laws, courts, the forming of States, the charters of
cities, the going and coming of commerce and
mails, are all for you.
....
Will the whole come back then?
Can each see signs of the best by a look in the look-
ing-glass? is there nothing greater or more?
Does all sit there with you, with the mystic unseen
soul?

Strange and hard that paradox true I give,
Objects gross and the unseen soul arc one.

House-building, measuring, sawing the boards,
Blacksmithing, glass-blowing, nail-making, coopering,
tin-roofing, shingle-dressing,
Ship-joining, dock-building, fish-curing, flagging of
sidewalks by flaggers,
The pump, the pile-driver, the great derrick, the coal-
kiln and brick-kiln,
....
The blast-furnace and the puddling-furnace, the loup-
lump at the bottom of the melt at last, the rolling-
mill, the stumpy bars of pig-iron, the strong, clean-
shaped T-rail for railroads,
....
The men and the work of men on ferries, railroad,
coasters, fish-boats, canals;

The hourly routine of your own or any man's life,
    the shop, yard, store, or factory,
These shows all near you by day and night—workman!
    whoever you are, your daily life!
In that and them the heft of the heaviest—in that and
    them far more than you estimated, (and far less
    also.)
....
I do not affirm that what you see beyond is futile, I do
    not advise you to stop,
I do not say leadings you thought great are not great,
But I say that none lead to greater than these lead to.

Will you seek afar off? you surely come back at last,
In things best known to you finding the best, or as
    good as the best,
In folks nearest to you finding the sweetest, strongest,
    lovingest,
Happiness, knowledge, not in another place but this
    place, not for another hour but this hour....

(1855–1881)[7]

    Not for another hour but for this hour...indeed, for this very mo-
ment. In the present, at this moment, in this place: this is the point
where contemplation and action meet. It is here, with "the sacrament
of the present moment," that we find and work our way back to
wholeness. The juncture of work and prayer is the time and place of
integrality. Here, where the means become the end, is also the
common ground between art and religion. As Eric Gill observes,

    The disinterestedness of the artist, the maker, the re-
    sponsible workman[woman] is the thing which makes
    him[her] friend and brother[sister] to the saint, the
    holy [person]. The saint is the disinterested [person];
    the artist is the disinterested workman[woman]. Their
    disinterestedness is their common ground....You can-
    not separate art and religion. The religious [person] is
    simply man[woman], the artist is simply religious

man[woman] turned workman[woman].[8]

It is how we do what we do that is important (not, of course, denying the fact that the "what" is also crucial). The Native American people have a profound understanding of the integrality of all of life as the following statement by an Oglala Lakota chief illuminates.

> We don't make any separation between religion and the rest of our life....There are special times of year when we have ceremonies or go into the hills to seek visions, but our real religion is living the right way every day. An Indian leader doesn't have any special privilege like in America or in Europe; an Indian leader lives like the rest of the people. We teach our children how to walk in a sacred manner on this earth; then there is no room in the society for evil.[9]

We, as Christians or Americans, or as whatever else we may happen to classify ourselves, could do no better. We also must learn "to walk in a sacred manner on this earth." We, too, must seek vision, vision to embrace our tasks. For, if people are "the visionary dreamers and mythmakers," then this aspect of ourselves has been drowned by that part of us "obsessed with *useful* work and rational activity, and we have lost the art of dreaming, of having visions, of imaging future possibilities quite different from that suggested by all the 'fact'."[10]

Now, then, is the time to break the bonds; to build a new world. Every day, in every moment and every action of our lives!

> Magical power,
>   marvelous action!
> Chopping wood,
>   carrying water...

NOTES

Chapter 1.
Toward a Practical Spirituality

[1]Rick Fields with Peggy Taylor, Rex Weyler, and Rick Ingrasci. *Chop Wood, Carry Water: A Guide to Finding Spiritual Fulfillment in Everyday Life* (Los Angeles: Jeremy P. Tarcher, Inc., 1984), p. xi.

[2]*The American Heritage Dictionary*, 1981 ed., S.v. "work," p. 1474.

[3]*The World Book Dictionary*, 1971 ed., S.v. "work," p. 2391.

[4]Chris Budden, "Theology of Work" (Manuscript draft, 1984), p. 5.

[5]Martha Graham, quoted in sermon by Eric Dale.

[6]Douglas Steere, *Work and Contemplation* (New York: Harper & Row, 1957), p. 8.

[7]Nikolai Berdyaev, quoted in James Gillespie, "Toward Freedom in Work," in George Benello and Dimitrios Roussopoulos, eds., *The Case for Participatory Democracy* (New York: Grossman Publishers, 1971), p. 76.

[8]Sigmund Freud, ibid., p. 77.

[9]*Ecclesiastes*, ibid.

[10]James Gillespie, "Toward Freedom in Work," ibid.

[11]Simone Weil, quoted in Clare B. Fischer, "The Fiery Bridge: Simone Weil's Theology of Work" (Ph.D. dissertation, Graduate Theological Union, 1979), p. 34.

[12]Ibid., p. 136.

[13]Hannah Arendt, *The Human Condition* (Chicago: The University of Chicago Press, 1958), p. 5.

[14]Ibid.

[15]Ibid., p. 7.

[16]Ibid., p. 136.

[17]Ibid.

[18]Ibid.

[19]Ibid., p. 7.

[20]Ibid., pp. 8, 9.

[21]Other people have also reflected on the difference between work and labor. Alasdair Clayre, in his book *Work and Play*, helps clarify the distinction with these two illustrations: "An artist can look back on his labours; he can look around at his work"; "A builder works, his hod-carrier labours" (p. 210). D. M. Dooling graphically points out the difference in reflecting on Simone Weil's factory work as her experience of "...her *work* becoming, [in effect], labor, her initiative of self-dedication and affirmation turning automatic, alien, oppressive 'in the circuit of inert matter'" (*A Way of Working*, p. 26).

[22]Arendt, *Human Condition*, p. 144.

[23]Ibid., pp. 143–44.

[24]Arendt, *Human Condition*, footnote on p. 146.

[25]The argument is often made, at this point, that this striving after such experiences is really only a case of abdicating one's identity, of somehow giving in to necessity, of giving up in the face of the real world; indeed, of turning away from the real world and the community

of people and becoming lost and isolated into "me, myself, and I." I find such an argument unconvincing. On the contrary, I think that without such times and opportunities for stopping the mind, for contemplating, for withdrawal into one's self (i.e., the SELF), a person can literally go mad; mad in the sense that "I" will never know who "I" am, "I" will never be centered or grounded, and as such will merely be re-acting from external stimuli rather than from the core of my being; the SELF.

[26]Jean Lacroix, "The Concept of Work," *Cross Currents* 4 (Spring-Summer 1954): 237.

[27]Ibid., p. 248. Author's emphasis.

[28]Ibid., p. 239.

[29]Ibid.

[30]Louis Savary, *Man: His World and His Work* (New York: Paulist Press, 1967), p. 177.

[31]Ibid., p. 178.

[32]Ibid.

[33]Ibid., p. 180.

[34]Ibid.

[35]Pope John Paul II uses the term "Man" throughout; I have substituted "Humanity."

[36]Pope John Paul II, *Laborem Exercens* 1981, quoted in Gregory Baum, *The Priority of Labor: A Commentary on "Laborem Exercens"* (New York: Paulist Press, 1982), p. 106.

[37]Ibid., pp. 141–42.

[38]D. M. Dooling, ed., *A Way of Working* (Garden City, New York:

Anchor Press/Doubleday, 1979), p. 61.

[39]Ibid., p. x.

[40]Ibid., p. i.

[41]Ibid.

[42]Steere, *Work and Contemplation*, p. 22.

[43]John Paul II, *Laborem Exercens* V. 24, pp. 141–42.

[44]*An Orthodox Approach to Diaconia*. Consultation on Church and Service, November 1978. World Council of Churches, Commission on Inter-Church Aid, Refugee and World Service (Geneva, Switzerland: World Council of Churches, 1980), p. 23.

[45]Steere, *Work and Contemplation*, p. 57.

[46]Saint Maximus the Confessor, quoted in M. D. Chenu, *The Theology of Work* (Chicago: Henry Regnery Co., 1966), pp. 111–12.

Chapter 2.
Spirituality

[1]Dates are from *The Oxford Dictionary of the Christian Church*, F. L. Cross and E. A. Livingstone, eds., 2nd ed. (London: Oxford University Press, 1974).

[2]Chenu, *Work*, p. 106.

[3]Ibid., pp. 107–08.

[4]Ibid., p. 109.

[5]Ibid., pp. 109–10.

[6]Maximus, quoted in Chenu, pp. 111–12.

[7]Chenu, *Work*, pp. 112–13.

[8]Dorothy Sölle, "Christians for Socialism," *Cross Currents* 25 (Winter 1976): 428–29.

[9]Ibid., p. 430.

[10]Ibid.

[11]Yusuf Ibish and Ileana Marculescu, eds., *Contemplation and Action in World Religions* (Huston, TX: Rothko Chapel, 1978).

[12]"Introduction," *The Philokalia*, vol. 1, Introduction, Translated and edited by G. E. M. Palmer, Philip Sherrard and Kallistos Ware (London: Faber & Faber, 1979), p. 14.

[13]Chenu, *Work*, p. 12.

[14]St. Mark the Ascetic, quoted in *Philokalia*, vol. 1, p. 86.

[15]Ibid., p. 126.

[16]Evelyn Underhill, *Mysticism* (New York: E. P. Dutton & Co., 1961), p. 50.

[17]Ibid., p. 81.

[18]*Staretz* is the Russian term for a spiritual father or director.

[19]Theophan the Recluse, quoted in I. Chartion, Compiler, E. Kadloubovsky and E. M. Palmer, trans., Timothy Ware, ed. and introd. *The Art of Prayer: An Orthodox Anthology* (London: Faber & Faber, 1966), pp. 235, 240.

[20]Steere, *Work and Contemplation*, p. 104.

[21]Ibid., p. 90.

[22]Claude J. Peifer, *The Elements of Monastic Spirituality* (New

York: Sheed and Ward, 1966), pp. 418–19.

[23]Ibid., p. 421.

[24]Cuthbert Butler, *Benedictine Monachism, Studies in Benedictine Life and Rule* (London: Longmans, Green & Co., 1919), p. 96.

[25]Ibid., pp. 93–101, 98.

[26]Ibid., pp. 99–100.

[27]Ibid., p. 100.

[28]Gregory the Great, "Homilies on Ezechiel," II, V, 19, quoted in Butler, *Benedictine Monachism*, p. 100.

[29]Ananda Coomaraswamy, *Christian and Oriental Philosophy of Art* (New York: Dover Publications, Inc., 1956), p. 137. Author's emphasis.

[30]Clement of Alexandria, *Protrepticus* or "An Exhortation to the Greeks," quoted in Forrester, *Christian Vocation*, p. 47.

[31]Steere, *Work and Contemplation*, pp. 11–12.

[32]Ibid., p. 12.

[33]St. Benedict, quoted in Anthony Meisel and Mihidel Mastro, trans. with intro. and notes, *The Rule of St. Benedict* (Garden City, New York: Image Books/Doubleday & Co., 1975), p. 86.

[34]Arthur T. Geoghegan, *The Attitude Toward Labor in Early Christianity and Ancient Culture* (Washington, DC: The Catholic University of America Press, 1945), p. 217.

[35]Owen Chadwick, trans. with intro. and notes, *Western Asceticism* (Philadelphia, PA: The Westminster Press. (The Library of Christian Classics), 1958), p. 27.

[36]Dom Rembert Sorg, *Towards a Benedictine Theology of Manual Work* (Lisle, IL: Benedictine Orient, 1951), p. 20.

[37]St. Benedict, quoted in Kenneth Kirk, *The Vision of God* (London: Longmans, Green & Co., 1931), p. 271.

[38]Kirk, *Vision of God*, p. 274.

[39]Geoghegan, *Attitude Toward Labor*, p. 218.

[40]Ibid., p. 231.

[41]Ibid., p. 219.

[42]St. Augustine, *De Opere Monachorum*, ch. 20, quoted in Geoghegan, p. 206.

[43]Steere, p. 109.

[44]St. Basil the Great, quoted in Geoghegan, p. 179.

[45]St. John Cassian, *Institutes* II, 14, quoted in Geoghegan, p. 214.

[46]St. Augustine, quoted in Geoghegan, p. 212.

[47]Geoghegan, p. 215.

[48]St. John Cassian, *Institutes*, quoted in Geoghegan, p. 215.

[49]Ibid.

[50]Sorg, *Manual Labor*, p. 36.

[51]Cassian defines *accidie*: "What the Greeks call 'Akedia' we call weariness or anxiety of heart." (*Institutes* 10, 1), quoted in Sorg, footnote #71, p. 48.

Chapter 3.
The Art of Working

[1]William Morris was born in 1834, and educated at Marlborough, Exeter College, and Oxford. Trained as an architect and painter, he became a poet, declining an offer for the chair of Professor of Poetry at Oxford, and general craftsman. He lectured on the arts, on crafts, and on socialism for the greater part of his life, and founded the Kelmscott Press in 1891. He died in 1896.

[2]Holbrook Jackson, "Introduction" to *On Art and Socialism*, by William Morris (Paulton, Somerset, and London: John Lehman Ltd., 1947), p. 7.

[3]Eric Gill, 1882–1940, the son of a non-establishment church minister (a preacher's kid), studied art for a couple of years before taking an apprenticeship in architecture. Prior to its full course, however, Gill sought employment as a stone and monument cutter, a field in which he continued to work throughout his life—and in which, arguably, his greatest works were done.

[4]Dorothy Sayers, 1893–1957, was a lay theologian and a playwright, in addition to being an author of well-known detective stories.

[5]Dorothy Sayers, "Why Work?" in *Creed or Chaos?* (London: Methuen & Co. Ltd., 1947), p. 46.

[6]Ibid.

[7]Gary Snyder, "Removing the Plate of the Pump on the Hydraulic System of the Backhoe," in *Axe Handles* (San Francisco: North Point Press, 1983), p. 93.

[8]Sayers, "Why Work?," pp. 58–59.

[9]Ibid., p. 62.

[10]William Morris, "Useful Work vs. Useless Toil," in *Art and Socialism*, p. 176.

[11]Morris, "The Art of the People," p. 53.

[12]Steere, *Work and Contemplation*, p. 8.

[13]Primary to Gill's understanding of the role of art in the human enterprise is the statement he uses from A.K. Coomaraswamy, "The artist is not a special kind of person, but every person is a special kind of artist." Gill defines Art as "the making of something with skill." Hence the relevance of *quality* in workmanship, if all would be artists. Though such a broad definition of art originally appealed to me, I have come to regard it with a touch of scepticism. I am not so sure that all people should be, or can be, considered or classified as artists.

I am convinced that there is a specialness, some kind of intentionality, about art; about artists. Art involves both this intentionality and a reflectiveness. Art is a reflective endeavor of representation. This rules out many (most?) people who work. However, if we define art as "skill," then the number of people included is larger; though we can still see that not everyone exhibits skill.

I still believe that the understanding of art as quality and the subsequent demand for personal responsibility are necessary ingredients for a renewal of meaningful work and whole/integral human lives and relationships. I am not so sure I would interpret art as broadly as does Gill.

[14]Ananda K. Coomaraswamy, quoted by Eric Gill in *Art* (London: The Bodley Head, 1934), p. 6.

[15]Eric Gill, *Art*, pp. 7–8.

[16]Morris, "Art and Its Producers," in *Art and Socialism*, pp. 209–10. Author's emphasis.

[17]"Art and craft are aspects (potential, not guaranteed) of all work that is undertaken intentionally and voluntarily; all work, in other words, that is worthily human, that is not 'donkey work' or drudgery, the labor of any animal of a machine. *Both art and craft must take part*

in any activity which has the power to transform" (D.M. Dowling, *The Way of Working*, pp. viii-ix. Emphasis added.).

[18]Eric Gill, "Work," in *It All Goes Together: Selected Essays* (Freeport, NY: Books for Libraries Press, 1971), p. 127.

[19]Morris, "The Aim of Art," in *Art and Socialism*, p. 84.

[20]Ibid., p. 90.

[21]Sayers, "Living to Work," in *Unpopular Opinions* (New York: Harcourt, Brace & Co., 1947), p. 125.

[22]Sayers, "Why Work?", p. 50.

[23]Ibid.

[24]Ibid., p. 54.

[25]Ibid.

[26]Sayers, "Living to Work," p. 126.

[27]Sayers, "Why Work?", p. 63.

[28]Gill, "The Nature of Art," in *Art*, p. 31.

[29]By this description I refer to all people anywhere in the world who have broken or are in the process of breaking ties with their cultural traditions, including religious traditions.

[30]Gill, Introduction to *The Hindu View of Art*, by Mulk Raj Anand (Bombay: Asia Publishing House, 1933), p. xviii.

[31]Karl Marx, "Alienated Labor," from *The Economic and Philosophic Manuscripts* (1844), in *Karl Marx: Early Writings*, ed. and trans. T. B. Bottomore (New York: McGraw-Hill Book Company, 1963), pp. 124–25.

[32]Antler, *Factory* (San Francisco: City Lights Books 1980), pp. 7, 10, 16.

[33]Gill, "The Factory System and Christianity" in *It All Goes Together*, pp. 26–27.

[34]Harry F. Ward, *Our Economic Morality and the Ethic of Jesus* (New York: The Macmillian Co., 1929), pp. 181–82.

[35]Carla Needleman, *The Work of Craft: An Inquiry into the Nature of Craft and Craftsmanship* (New York: Alfred A. Knopf, 1979), p. 55.

[36]Ibid., p. 57.

[37]Ibid.

[38]Ibid.

[39]Hence the term "artisans" which I will use both to designate the marriage and because of its inclusive tone, gender-wise.

[40]Arendt, *Human Condition*, pp. 210–11.

[41]*The Way of Chang Tzu*, trans. Thomas Merton, quoted in Joan Bodner, ed., *Taking Charge of Our Lives* (San Francisco: Harper & Row, 1984), pp. 12–13.

[42]Jacob Needleman, *Consciousness and Tradition* (New York: Crossroad, 1982), p. 4.

[43]*The Bhagavad Gita*, trans. Swami Nikhilananda (New York: Ramakrishna-Vivekananda Center, 1952), p. 107.

[44]Ibid., p. 112.

[45]Swami Vivekananda, *Karma Yoga* (Calcutta, India; Advaita Ashrama, 1974), pp. 38, 46–47.

[46]Ibid., p. 11.

⁴⁷Ibid., p. 8.

⁴⁸Ibid., p. 22.

⁴⁹Ben Shahn, *The Shape of Content* (Cambridge, Massachusetts: Harvard University Press, 1957), pp. 79–81.

⁵⁰Gill, "Art and Holiness," in *Art*, p. 128.

⁵¹Ibid., p. 129.

⁵²Walt Whitman, "I Hear America Singing," in *Leaves of Grass*, ed. Emory Holloway (Garden City, New York: Blue Ribbon Books, 1942), p. 10.

⁵³Ibid.

⁵⁴Vivekananda, *Work and Its Secrets*, pp. 26-27.

⁵⁵Theophan quoted in *The Art of Prayer*, p. 240.

⁵⁶Emmanuel Heufelder, OSB., *The Way to God According to the Rule of Saint Benedict*, trans. Luke Eberle, OSB (Kalamazoo, MI: Cistercians Publications, 1983), p. 211.

⁵⁷Sorg, *Manual Labor*, p. 87.

⁵⁸Ibid., pp. 89–90.

⁵⁹St. Jerome, "Epistola XVI," n. 11, quoted in Sorg, *Manual Labor*, p. 90.

⁶⁰Edwin Kaiser, *Theology of Work* (1966). Josef Pieper, *In Tune with the World* (1973).

⁶¹Kaiser, *Theology of Work*, p. 460.

⁶²Ibid., p. 457.

[63]Ibid., p. 461.

[64]Steere, *Work and Contemplation*, p. 129.

[65]Gill, "Art," in *It All Goes Together*, p. 115.

[66]St. Paul, "Colossians," quoted in Geoghegan, *Attitude Towards Labor*, p. 196.

[67]Gill, "Art," *It All Goes Together*, p. 121.

[68]Sorg, *Manual Labor*, p. 27.

[69]Ibid., p. 29.

[70]St. Jerome, quoted in Steere, *Work and Contemplation*, p. 108.

[71]St. John Cassian, quoted in Geoghegan, *Attitude Towards Labor*, p. 216.

[72]St. Basil, quoted in Sorg, *Manual Labor*, p. 30.

[73]Ram Das, quoted in Rick Fields et al., eds., *Chop Wood, Carry Water*, p. 107.

[74]Ibid.

[75]Emil Brunner, *Christianity and Civilization*, vol. 2.

[76]Ibid.

[77]Gill, *Art*, p. 20.

[78]Ibid., p. 21.

[79]Ibid., p. 22.

[80]Sayers, "Why Work?", p. 55.

[81]Ibid., p. 57.

[82]Ibid., p. 59.

[83]Kenneth Kirk, *The Vision of God* (London: Longmans, Green & Co., 1931), p. 447.

[84]Ibid.

[85]Ibid., p. 451.

Chapter 4.
The Socio-Ethic of Spiritual Work

[1]Mahatma Gandhi, quoted in *A Guide to Prayer for Ministers and Other Servants*, Rueben P. Job and Norman Shawchuck (Nashville, TN: The Upper Room, 1983), p. 234.

[2]Morris, "The Lesser Arts," in *William Morris*, ed. G.D.H. Cole (London: The Nonesuch Press, 1948), p. 497.

[3]Ibid., p. 515.

[4]I emphasize the Benedictine tradition, simply because I am more familiar with it.

[5]W. R. Forrester, *Christian Vocation: Studies in Faith and Work* (New York: Charles Scribner's Sons, 1953), pp. 20–21.

[6]John Paul II, *Laborem Exercens*, p. 105.

[7]Brunner, *Christianity and Civilization*, p. 58.

[8]Arendt, *Human Condition*, p. 81. Arendt reminds us, however, that "Historically, it is important to keep in mind the distinction between the contempt of the Greek city-states for all non-political occupations which arose out of the enormous demands upon the time and energy of the citizens, and the earlier, more original, and more

general contempt for activities which serve only to sustain life..."
(Ibid., footnote #7, pp. 82–83).

⁹John Paul II, *Laborem Exercens*, p. 106.

¹⁰Ibid.

¹¹Forrester, *Christian Vocation*, p. 119. The soteriological question, i.e., what we are meant to be, will have to wait until later in this section.

¹²John Paul II, *Laborem Exercens*, p. 104.

¹³Chenu, *Work*, p. 106

¹⁴Ibid.

¹⁵Ibid., pp. 105–06.

¹⁶Ibid, p. 23.

¹⁷Ibid.

¹⁸Ibid., p. 24.

¹⁹Ibid., p. 23.

²⁰Baum, *Priority of Labor*, p. 17.

²¹National Conference of Catholic Bishops, *Pastoral Letter on Catholic Social Teaching and the U.S. Economy*, First draft (Washington, DC: National Conference of Catholic Bishops, 1984), I.B. 70, pp. 3, 9.

²²Ibid., I.1.27.

²³E. F. Schumacher, *Good Work* (New York: Harper & Row, 1979), p. 122.

²⁴Ignazio Silone, *Bread and Wine*, trans. Harvey Fergusson III, with an Afterward by Marc Slonim (New York: Harper & Brothers, 1937; reprint ed., New York: The New American Library, 1963), pp. 269–70.

²⁵Clement of Alexandria, *Protrepticus*, x, quoted in Forrester, *Christian Vocation*, p. 47.

²⁶Forrester, *Christian Vocation*, p. 20.

²⁷Ibid., p. 21.

²⁸I take good to mean more than "not bad," in the sense of good and evil. It includes that but I think the emphasis is on the sense of completeness, wholeness, "well done!"

²⁹cf. Coomaraswamy, *Philosophy of Art*, p. 137: "In traditional society any and all functions (*svadharma*), however 'menial' or 'commercial', is strictly speaking a 'way' (*marga*), so that it is not by engaging in other work to which a higher or lower social prestige may attach, but to the extent that a man [or a woman] approaches perfection in his [or her] own work and understands its spiritual significance that he [or she] can *rise above himself [or herself]*—an ambition to *rise above his [or her] fellows* having then no longer any meaning." (author's emphasis).

³⁰The above assertions lead me to make a distinction between what I shall call the metaphysical reality and the perceived reality. That the workplace is sacramental is the metaphysical reality: all creation is sacred, i.e., of God. That the workplace is not understood or seen to be sacramental in peoples' lives is the perceived reality: peoples' ideas and perceptions do not include the understanding of the sacredness of all creation, and thus, for them, in their daily lives (i.e., their field of perception), it is not so.

³¹This transformation is of the magnitude of a cultural or paradigm shift; with it we are talking about conversion; we are talking about aligning our perceived reality with metaphysical reality; we are talking about walking in God's way, in harmony with the earth: doing

justice, loving kindness, and walking humbly with God.

[32]Vivekananda, *Work*, pp. 5 and 6.

[33]Yves Simon, *Work, Society, and Culture*, ed. Vukan Kuic (New York: Fordham University Press, 1971), p. 71.

[34]Marx, "Alienated Labor," pp. 124–25.

[35]Baum, *Priority of Labor*, p. 46f.

[36]Ibid., p. 69.

[37]Ibid., p. 85.

[38]Dooling, *Way of Working*, p. viii.

[39]Also see pg. 46, note #15, and pg. 49, note #19.

[40]Dooling, *Way of Working*, pp. 99–100.

[41]Joseph Fletcher, ed., *Christianity and Property* (Philadelphia: The Westminster Press, 1947), p. 175.

[42]U.S. Bishops, First draft—*Pastoral on the Economy*, I.3.51.

[43]Vida Scudder, "Anglican Thought on Property," in *Christianity and Property*, p. 149.

[44]U.S. Bishops, *Pastoral on the Economy*, I.1.29.

[45]Harry F. Ward, *Our Economic Morality and the Ethic of Jesus* (New York: The Macmillan Co., 1929), p. 18.

[46]U.S. Bishops, *Pastoral on the Economy*, I.B.69.

[47]Ibid.

[48]Ibid., B.70.

[49]Ibid.

[50]*Orthodox Approach to Diaconia*, p. 25.

[51]Ibid.

[52]Ibid., p. 18.

[53]The Cappadocian Fathers, i.e., St. Basil the Great, St. Gregory of Nyssa, and St. Gregory of Nazianzen, gave grounding in overcoming dualism. Ibid., p. 23.

[54]Solle, "Christianity and Socialism," p. 424.

[55]Ibid., p. 429.

[56]Ibid., p. 430.

[57]*Orthodox Approach to Diaconia*, p. 22.

[58]"Tarthang Talku Rinpoche is a religious teacher from Tarthang Monastery in East Tibet. During his early life in Tibet he received a thorough education in the philosophy and practice of Tibetan Buddhism.... In 1959 he left Tibet and went to India where he taught at Sanskrit University in Benares for seven years.... In 1969 he founded the Tibetan Nyingma Meditation Center (in the United States)." (*Skillful Means*, "About the Author,"), p. 133.

[59]Tarthang Talku, *Skillful Means* (Berkeley, CA: Dharma Publishing, 1978), p. 114.

[60]Ibid., p. 117.

[61]Ibid., pp. 119–20.

[62]Ibid., p. 121.

[63]Ibid., pp. 121–22. Emphasis added.

⁶⁴Ibid., p. 124.

⁶⁵Steere, *Work and Contemplation*, p. 127.

⁶⁶Ibid., p. 125.

⁶⁷Contemporary examples of women reflecting on the relation-ship of humans and nature are (1) *God's Fierce Whimsy: Christian Feminism and Theological Education*, by the Mud Flower Collective (New York: Pilgrim Press, 1985), and (2) Letty Russell, *Human Liberation in a Feminist Perspective—A Theology* (Philadelphia: The Westminster Press, 1974).

⁶⁸Julian of Norwich (c. 1342–after 1413). "English mystic. Little known of her life except that she probably lived as an anchoress, outside the walls of St. Julian's Church, Norwich. *The 16 Revelations of Divine Love* was written 20 years after, as the fruit of her meditations on the original experience [on 8 and 9 May 1373, by her own account], which consisted chiefly in visions of the Passion and the Holy Trinity." (*The Oxford Dictionary of the Christian Church*, 2nd ed., 1974, pp. 766–67.)

St. Hildegard (1098–1179) of Bingen. Abbess of Rupertsberg, near Bingen (in the Rhineland). "Benedictine nun, ...subject to super-natural religious experiences from early childhood.... Seems to have exerted a wide influence, numbering...various kings, prelates, and saints among her correspondents." Some of her writings "...reflect a degree of scientific observation unusual in medieval times." She was canonized in the 15th century. Her feast day is 17 September (Ibid., p. 750).

⁶⁹The bearing of children, obviously, being restricted to women.

⁷⁰Morris, "The Beauty in Life," in *Art and Socialism*, p. 57.

⁷¹Ibid.

⁷²A "joinery" of the two: "From the same word which is the root of

'art' and 'order' comes the carpenter's word for 'joinery' in Greek, *harmos*, from which comes 'harmony'." *A Way of Working*, p. x.

[73]Morris, "The Beauty in Life," p. 59.

[74]Morris, "The Art of the People," in *Art and Socialism*, p. 54.

[75]Morris, "The Beauty in Life," p. 73.

[76]Ibid., p. 75.

[77]Morris, *Nonesuch*, quoted in A. Clayre, *Work and Play*, p. 75.

Epilogue

[1]*UME Connexion*, 1984, p. 11.

[2]Ram Das, quoted in Rick Fields, et al., *Chop Wood, Carry Water*, p. xii.

[3]Gill, "Work and Culture," in *Sacred & Secular & C*, p. 120.

[4]Steere, *Work and Contemplation*, p. 81f.

[5]Gill, "Art in England Now...As It Seems to Me," in *It All Goes Together*, p. 93.

[6]Gill, "Private Property," pp. 129–30.

[7]Walt Whitman, "A Song for Occupations," *Leaves of Grass*, ed. Emory Holloway (Garden City, NY: Blue Ribbon Books, 1942), pp. 179–85.

[8]Gill, *Art*, p. 128.

[9]Matthew King, Oglala Lakota Chief, quoted in Fields, *Chop Wood, Carry Water*, pp. 245–46.

[10]Chris Budden, "Theology of Work," (manuscript draft), chapter 2, p. 6.

SELECT BIBLIOGRAPHY

I. VOCATION AND WORK

Apprentice Alliance. *Directory*. San Francisco: Apprentice Alliance, 1985. (II) (Numbers in parentheses indicate relationship to additional categories.)

Billing, Einar. *Our Calling*. Translated by Conrad Bergendoff. Abridged edition by Campus Ministry Communications, Lutheran Council in the USA, Chicago, Illinois, 1979. (1909, Swedish pub.; 1947, English).

Calhoun, Robert L. *God and the Day's Work: Christian Vocation in an UnChristian World*. New York: Association Press, 1957.

Dale, Alfred S., Jr. "Life-Style: Christians Being in the World." D. Rel. position paper, Chicago Theological Seminary, 1969. (III, IV)

Forrester, W. R. *Christian Vocation: Studies in Faith and Work*. New York: Charles Scribner's Sons, 1953.

Heiges, Donald R. *The Christian's Calling*. Rev. ed. Philadelphia: Fortress Press, 1984.

Kee, Howard C., and Shroyer, Montgomery J. *The Bible and God's Call*. The Methodist Church Interboard Committee on Christian Vocation and the Department of Ministerial Education, 1962.

Laymen's Work. A bulletin issued by the Secretary for Laymen's Work, World Council of Churches, Geneva, Switzerland, Volumes 1–8, May 1951–Spring 1955.

Nelson, John Oliver, ed. *Work and Vocation*. New York: Harper, 1954.

Trueblood, Elton. *Your Other Vocation.* New York: Harper & Bros., 1952.

II. WORK AND THE SPIRITUALITY OF EVERYDAY LIVING

The Art of Prayer: An Orthodox Anthology. Compiled by I. Chartion of Valamo. Translated by E. Kadloubovsky and E. M. Palmer. Edited with introduction by Timothy Ware. London: Faber & Faber, Ltd., 1966. (III)

Beitz, Charles, and Washburn, Michael. *Creating the Future: A Guide to Living and Working for Social Change.* New York: Bantam Books, 1974.

Bodner, Joan, ed. *Taking Charge of Our Lives: Living Responsibly in the World.* (American Friends Service Committee, San Francisco). San Francisco: Harper & Row, 1984.

Chadwick, Owen, Translator with Introduction and notes. *Western Asceticism.* The Library of Christian Classics. Philadelphia, PA: The Westminster Press, 1958. (III)

Dooling, D. M. "Alchemy and Craft." *Parabola 3* (August 1978): 24–29. (V)

Dooling, D. M., ed. *A Way of Working.* Garden City, NY: Anchor Press/Doubleday, 1979. (V)

Fields, Rick, with Taylor, Peggy; Weyler, Rex; and Ingrasci, Rick. *Chop Wood, Carry Water: A Guide to Finding Spiritual Fulfillment in Everyday Life.* Los Angeles: Jeremy P. Tarcher, Inc., 1984.

Fosdick, Harry Emerson. *The Meaning of Prayer.* Introduction by John R. Mott. New York: Association Press, 1916.

_____. *The Meaning of Service.* New York: Association Press, 1921.

Muktananda, Swami. *Where Are You Going? A Guide to the Spiritual Journey.* South Fallsburg, New York: SYDA Foundation, 1981.

_____. *I Have Become Alive: Secrets of the Inner Journey.* South Fallsburg, New York: SYDA Foundation, 1985.

Needleman, Jacob, ed. *Speaking of My Life: The Art of Living in the Cultural Revolution.* San Francisco: Harper & Row, 1979. (V)

Phillips, Michael, and Rasberry, Salli. *Honest Business.* New York: Random House, 1981.

The Philokalia, 2 vols. Translated by G. E. H. Palmer, Philip Sherrard, and Kallistos Ware. Boston: Faber and Faber, 1979 (vol. 1), 1981 (vol. 2). (III)

Purdy, John C. *Parables at Work.* Philadelphia: The Westminster Press, 1985.

The Rule of Saint Benedict. Translated, with Introduction and notes by Anthony C. Meisel and M. L. del Mastro. Garden City, NY: Doubleday and Co., Image Books, 1975. (III)

Tulku, Tarthang. *Skillful Means.* Berkeley, CA: Dharma Publishing, 1978.

Underhill, Evelyn. *Mysticism.* New York: E. P. Dutton & Co., 1961 (1911). (III)

Vivekananda, Swami. *Work and Its Secret.* Calcutta, India: Advaita Ashrama, 1976. (III)

The Way of a Pilgrim and *The Pilgrim Continues His Way.* Translated by R. M. French. New York: Ballantine Books, 1974. (V)

III. PHILOSOPHICAL AND THEOLOGICAL ASPECTS OF WORK

Agrell, Goran. *Work, Toil, and Sustenance: An Examination of the View of Work in the New Testament Taking into Consideration Views Found in Old Testament, Intertestamental, and Early Rabbinic Writings.*Lund, Sweden: Verbum, Hakan Ohlssons Forlag, 1976.

Arendt, Hannah. *The Human Condition.* Chicago: The University of Chicago Press, 1958.

Avila, Charles. *Ownership: Early Christian Teaching.* New York: Orbis Books, 1983. (IV)

Baum, Gregory. *The Priority of Labor: A Commentary on "Laborem exercens."* Encyclical Letter of Pope John Paul II. New York: Paulist Press, 1982. (IV)

Baum, Gregory, ed. *Work and Religion* (Concilium 131, 1/1980). New York: The Seabury Press, 1980.

Berry, Thomas. "Wonderworld as Wasteworld: The Earth in Deficit." *Cross Currents* 35 (Winter 1985–86): 408–22. (IV)

The Bhagavad Gita. Translated with notes, comments, and introduction by Swami Nikhilananda. New York: Ramakrishna-Vivekananda Center, 1952. (II)

Brunner, Emil. *Christianity and Civilization.* Second Part: *Specific Problems.* New York: Charles Scribner's Sons, 1949. (Especially Chapter 5, "Work," pp. 57–71). (IV)

Buckley, Mark D. "Personalism." *Religious Socialism* 10 (Spring 1986): 1, 7–9. (IV)

Budden, Chris. *Theology of Work.* Manuscript draft. N/D.

Burckhardt, Titus. *Alchemy: Science of the Cosmos, Science of the*

Soul. Translated by William Stoddart. Baltimore, MD: Penguin Books Inc., 1971. (*Alchemie* published originally by Walter-Verlag Ag, Olten, 1960). (V)

Butler, Cuthbert. *Benedictine Monachism, Studies in Benedictine Life and Rule.* London: Longmans, Green & Co., 1919.

Chenu, M. D., O.P. *The Theology of Work.* Translated by Lilian Soiron. Chicago: Henry Regnery Co., 1966.

Clayre, Alasdair. *Work and Play: Ideas and Experience of Work and Leisure.* New York: Harper & Row, 1974.

Coomaraswamy, Ananda K. *Christian and Oriental Philosophy of Art.* New York: Dover Publications, Inc., 1956 (1943). (V)

Ducey, M. "The Benedictines and Manual Labor." *American Benedictine Review* 1 (1950): 467–89. (II)

Ellul, Jacques. "From the Bible to a History of Non-Work." *Cross Currents* 35 (Spring 1985): 43–48.

Fiorenza, Francis Schussler. "Religious Beliefs and Praxis: Reflections on Catholic Theological Views of Work." In *Religion and Work* (Concilium 131), pp. 92–102. Edited by Gregory Baum. New York: The Seabury Press, 1980.

Fischer, Clare B. "The Fiery Bridge: Simone Weil's Theology of Work." Ph.D. dissertation, Graduate Theological Union, 1979.

Fletcher, Joseph F., ed. *Christianity and Property.* Philadelphia: The Westminster Press, 1947. (IV)

Forell, George W., and Lazareth, William H., eds. *Work as Praise.* Philadelphia: Fortress Press, 1979. (IV, I)

Geoghegan, Arthur T. *The Attitude Towards Labor in Early Christianity and Ancient Culture.* Dissertation series. Washington, DC: The Catholic University of America Press, 1945. (IV)

Hellman, John. "John Paul II and the Personalist Movement." *Cross Currents* 30 (Winter 1980–81): 409–419. (IV)

Heufelder, Emmanuel, O.S.B. *The Way to God According to the Rule of Saint Benedict*. Translated by Luke Eberle, O.S.B. Kalamazoo, MI: Cistercians Publications, 1983.

Ibish, Yusuf, and Marculescu, Illeada, eds.*Contemplation and Action in World Religions*. Houston: Rothko Chapel, 1978. (II)

Illich, Ivan. *Tools for Conviviality*. New York: Harper & Row, 1973. (IV)

Kaiser, Edwin G. *Theology of Work*. Westminster, MD: The Newman Press, 1966.

Kirk, Kenneth E. *The Vision of God*. London: Longmans, Green & Co., 1931.

Lacroix, Jean. "The Concept of Work." *Cross Currents* 4 (Spring–Summer 1954): 236–50.

Lascaris, Andrew, O.P. "Economics and Human Desire." *New Blackfriars* 68 (March 1987): 115–25. (IV)

Leclercq, Jean. "Benedictine Rule and Active Presence in the World." *Monastic Studies* 2 (1964): 51–63.

Leclercq, Jean, Vandenbroucke, F., and Bouer, Louis. *The History of Christian Spirituality*. Vol. 2: The Spirituality of the Middle Ages. London: Burn Oates, 1968; New York: Seabury, 1968.

Maximus Confessor, Selected Writings. Translated and notes by George C. Berthold. Introduction by Jaroslav Pelikan. Preface by Irenee-Henri Dalmais, O.P. The Classics of Western Spirituality. New York: Paulist Press, 1985.

Nasr, Seyyed Hossein. *Man and Nature: The Spiritual Crisis of Modern*

Man. London: George Allen & Unwin Ltd., Unwin Paperbacks, 1968.

National Conference of Catholic Bishops. First and Second Drafts— *Pastoral Letter on Catholic Social Teaching and the U.S. Economy*. Washington, DC: National Conference of Catholic Bishops, November 1984, and October 1985. (IV)

New Catholic Encyclopedia, 1967. S.v. "Mystical Body of Christ," by F. X. Lawlor.

_____. S.v. "Work, Theology of," by E. G. Kaiser.

An Orthodox Approach to Diaconia. Consultation on Church and Service (November 1978). World Council of Churches, Commission on Inter-Church Aid, Refugee and World Service. Geneva, Switzerland: World Council of Churches, 1980.

Peifer, Claude J., O.S.B. *Monastic Spirituality*. New York: Sheed & Ward, 1966.

Pieper, Josef. *In Tune with the World: A Theory of Festivity*. Translated by Richard and Clara Winston. New York: Harcourt, Brace and World, Inc., 1965; reprint ed., Chicago: Franciscan Herald Press, 1973.

Pohier, Jacques, and Mieth, Dietmar, eds. *Unemployment and the Right to Work*. (*Concilium* 160) (10/1982). New York: The Seabury Press, 1982. (IV)

Pope John Paul II. "Growing Difficulties in Work." *The Pope Speaks* 32 (Summer 1987): 115–20. (IV)

_____. *Laboren Exercens*, Encyclical Letter of Pope John Paul II. September 14, 1981. In *The Priority of Labor*, pp. 93–152. Gregory Baum. New York: Paulist Press, 1982. (IV)

_____. "Solidarity of Workers." *The Pope Speaks* 32 (Summer 1987): 121–25. (IV)

_____. "Solidarity Between People." *The Catholic Worker* (August 1987). (Excerpts from a homily given in Gdansk).

Rauschenbusch, Walter. *A Theology for the Social Gospel.* Nashville, TN: Abingdon, 1945.

Rerum Novarum, Encyclical Letter of His Holiness Pope Leo XIII on the Condition of the Working Classes. (1891).

Savary, Louis M. *Man, His World and His Work.* New York: Paulist Press, 1967. (IV)

Sayers, Dorothy. *Creed or Chaos?* London: Methuen & Co., Ltd., 1947. (Especially "Why Work?", pp. 46–62. (IV, V)

_____. "Living to Work." *Unpopular Opinions.* New York: Harcourt, Brace & Co., 1947.

_____. *The Mind of the Maker.* New York: Meridian Books, Living Age Books, 1956.

Schmemann, Alexander. *Sacraments and Orthodoxy.* New York: Herder & Herder, 1965.

Simon, Yves R. *Work, Society, and Culture.* Edited by Vukan Kuic. New York: Fordham University Press, 1971.

Sorg, Dom Rembert, O.S.B. *Towards a Benedictine Theology of Manual Labor.* Lisle, IL: Benedictine Orient, 1951.

Sri Krishna Prem. *The Yoga of the Bhagavat Gita.* Baltimore, MD: Penguin Books, 1973. (II)

St. Maximus the Confessor. *The Ascetic Life* and *The Four Centuries on Charity.* Translated and Annotated by Polycarp Sherwood. Ancient Christian Writers, No. 21. Westminster, MD: The Newman Press, 1955.

Steere, Douglas V. *On Beginning from Within.* New York: Harper & Brothers, 1943. (I, II)

_____. *Work and Contemplation.* New York: Harper & Row, 1957. (I, II)

Theological Dictionary of the New Testament, 1964 ed. S.v. "ἔργον, ἐργάζομαι" (English "work" and German "Werk"). Translated and edited by Geoffrey W. Bromiley, 9 vols. (Grand Rapids, MI: Wm. B. Eerdmans, 1964–1974).

A Theological Reflection on Economic and Labor Justice. Published by SEPI, the Social, Economic, and Political Task Force of the Commission on Religion in Appalachia (CORA). N/D.

Tilgher, Adriano. *Work: What It Has Meant to Men Through the Ages (Homo Faber).* Translated by Dorothy Canfield Fisher. New York: Harcourt, Brace and Company, 1958. (IV)

Troeltsch, Ernst. *The Social Teaching of the Christian Churches,* Vol. 1. Translated by Olive Wyon, Introduction by H. Richard Niebuhr. New York: Harper and Brothers, 1960 (1911, German ed.). (IV)

Vivekananda, Swami. *Karma-Yoga.* Calcutta: Advaita Ashrama, 1974 (15th impression). (II)

Walton, Gilbert. "The Process of Making." *The Modern Churchman* 24 (Autumn/Winter 1981): 171–77.

Ward, Harry F. *The Social Creed of the Churches.* New York: The Abingdon Press, 1914. (IV)

_____. *Our Economic Morality and the Ethic of Jesus.* New York: The Macmillan Co., 1929. (Especially Chapter Six, "The Chief End of Man," pp. 181–237, being an analysis of property and ownership). (IV)

_____. *Which Way Religion?* New York: The Macmillan Company, 1931. (IV)

Ware, Kallistos Timothy. "The Transfiguration of the Body." In *Sacrament and Image: Essays in the Christian Understanding of Man*, pp. 171. Edited by A. M. Allchin. London: Fellowship of St. Alban and St. Sergius, 1967.

Weil, Simone. "Factory Work." *Cross Currents* 25 (Winter 1976): 367–82.

Work and Justice: A Working Paper. Northwest Interfaith Movement, Philadelphia, Pennsylvania, Winter 1984.

Workman, Herbert B. *The Evolution of the Monastic Ideal.* Boston: Beacon Press, 1962. Originally published 1913.

IV. SOCIAL, POLITICAL, ECONOMIC, AND HISTORICAL ASPECTS OF WORK

Aronowitz, Stanley; Baran, Barbara; Breidenbach, Jan; Clark, Jack; and Harrington, Michael. "New Directions for the U.S. Labor Movement." *Democratic Left* 13 (July–October, 1985).

Bell, Daniel. *Work and Its Discontents: The Cult of Efficiency in America.* New York: League for Industrial Democracy, 1970 (originally published in 1956).

Bellah, Robert. Testimony before U.S. Catholic Bishops; published as "Work as Calling: Economics and the Theology of Work." *UME Connexion*, 1985. (Originally in *The New Oxford Review*, November 1984). (III)

Benello, C. George, and Roussopoulos, Dimitrios, eds. *The Case for Participatory Democracy: Some Prospects for a Radical Society.* New York: Grossman Publishers, 1971.

Carnoy, Martin, and Shearer, Derek. *Economic Democracy: The*

Challenge of the 1980s. Armonk, NY: M. E. Sharpe, Inc., 1980.

The Chesterton Review 8 (November 1982): 283–358. Special issue on Eric Gill. (III, IV)

Cunningham, Angela. "The Nature of Work in the Thought of Eric Gill and Vincent McNabb." *The Chesterton Review* 11 (August 1985): 295–306. (III)

"Economic Justice." *Faithful Witness on Today's Issues.* Washington, DC: The General Board of Church and Society of the United Methodist Church, 1984. (III)

Edwards, Richard. *Contested Terrain: The Transformation of the Workplace in the Twentieth Century.* New York: Basic Books, Inc., Harper, 1979.

Ehrenreich, Barbara, and Ehrenreich, John. "Work and Consciousness." *Technology, the Labor Process, and the Working Class,* pp. 10–18. New York: Monthly Review Press, 1976.

Ewing, David. "Free Speech Within the Corporation." In *The Big Business Reader: On Corporate America,* pp. 293–303. Edited by Mark Green. New York: The Pilgrim Press, 1983.

Freundlich, Paul; Collins, Chris; and Wenig, Mike. *A Guide to Cooperative Alternatives.* New Haven, CT: Community Publications Cooperative, 1979.

Fromm, Erich. *The Sane Society.* Greenwich, CT: Fawcett Publications, Inc., 1955. (III)

Gerth, H. H., and Mills, C. Wright, eds., translators, and introduction. *From Max Weber: Essays in Sociology.* New York: Oxford University Press, 1946.

Gillett, Richard W. *The Human Enterprise: A Christian Perspective on Work.* Kansas City, MO: Leaven Press, 1985.

Gneuhs, Geoffrey. "Worker Ownership." *The Catholic Worker*, 51 (December 1984): 1 & 8.

Honingsberg, Peter Jan; Kamoroff, Bernard; and Beaty, Jim. *We Own It: Starting and Managing Coops, Collectives and Employee-Owned Ventures*. Laytonville, CA: Bell Springs Publishing, 1982.

Jones, Barry. *Sleepers, Wake!: Technology and the Future of Work*. Melbourne, Australia: Oxford University Press, 1982.

Link, Eugene P. *Labor-Religion Prophet: The Times and Life of Harry F. Ward*. Foreword by Corliss Lamont. Illustrated by Lynd Ward. Boulder, CO: Westview Press, 1984.

Mumford, Lewis. *Technics and Civilization*. New York: Harcourt, Brace & World, Inc., 1963 (1934). (III)

Ogle, George. "Victory for Corporations, Defeat for Unions, Challenge for Churches." *e/sa engage/social action* 15 (November 1987): 10–31.

Pemberton, Prentiss L., and Finn, Daniel Rush. *Toward a Christian Economic Ethic: Stewardship and Social Power*. Minneapolis, MN: Winston Press, Inc., 1985.

Schumacher, E. F. *Small Is Beautiful: Economics as if People Mattered*. New York: Harper & Row, 1973. (III)

_____. *Good Work*. New York: Harper & Row, 1979. (II, III)

"Social Principles." *The Book of Discipline of the United Methodist Church*. Nashville, TN: The United Methodist Publishing House, 1984. (III)

Sölle, Dorothy. "Christians for Socialism." *Cross Currents* 25 (Winter 1976): 419–34. (III)

Terkel, Studs. *Working*. New York: Avon Books, 1972, 1974. (V)

"Unemployment." *e/sa engage/social action* (June 1983): 9-40.

Ward, Harry F. *The New Social Order: Principles and Programs*. New York: The Macmillan Company, 1920.

"Work in America." *Democratic Left* 14 (Sept.–Oct. 1986). Special issue focusing on "Women and Labor."

Work in America. Report of a Special Task Force to the Secretary of Health, Education, and Welfare. Foreword by Elliot Richardson. Cambridge, MA: The MIT Press, 1973.

Zwerdling, Daniel. *Workplace Democracy*. New York: Harper & Row, 1980 (1978).

V. LITERARY AND ARTISTIC ASPECTS OF WORK

Antler. *Factory*. San Francisco: City Lights Books, 1980.

Apostolos-Cappadona, Diane, ed. *Art, Creativity, and the Sacred: An Anthology in Religion and Art*. New York: Crossroad, 1984.

Coomaraswamy, Ananda K. *The Transformation of Nature in Art*. New York: Dover Publications, 1956 (1934). (III)

Dyrness, Bill. "Gathering Manna on Sunday." *The Other Side* (December 1982): 13–15. (III)

Foner, Philip S., and Schultz, Reinhard. *The Other America: Art and the Labour Movement in the United States*. London: The Journeyman Press, Ltd., 1985.

Gill, Eric. *Beauty Looks After Herself*. London: Sheed & Ward, 1933. (II, III)

_____. *Art*. London: The Bodley Head, 1934.

_____. "Art and Reality." Introductory Essay in *The Hindu View of Art*, pp. xi–xix. Anand, Mulk Raj. Bombay: Asia Publishing House, 1933. (III)

_____. *Christianity and the Machine Age*. London: The Sheldon Press, 1940. (III, IV)

_____. *Sacred and Secular & C.* London: J. M. Dent & Sons, Ltd., 1940. (II, III)

_____. *It All Goes Together: Selected Essays*. Freeport, NY: Books for Libraries Press, 1971 (reprint), 1944. (II, III)

_____. *Letters of Eric Gill*. Edited by Walter Shewring. London: Jonathon Cape, 1947.

Gilliam, Robert. "Re-Integrating Earth and Heaven." *The Catholic Worker*, August 1985, p. 5. (IV)

Hoffmann-Ogier, Wayne H. "Cutting the Crystal: The Spiritual Dimensions of the Creative Process." *Studia Mystica* 5 (Fall 1982): 3–25.

Hyde, Lewis. *The Gift: Imagination and the Erotic Life of Property*. New York: Vintage Books (Random House), 1979.

L'Engle, Madeleine. "Reflections on Faith and Art." *The Other Side* (December 1982): 10–12.

Leaves of Grass: The Collected Poems of Walt Whitman. Edited by Emory Holloway. Garden City, NY: Blue Ribbon Books, 1942. (Especially "A Song for Occupations," 1855–1881, pp. 179–85.).

Manno, Jack. "Syracuse Cultural Workers Project." *Communities*, Winter 1983/84, pp. 29–33. (II)

Michau, Raoul. "Interior Vision in Creative Art." *Studia Mystica* 3 (Summer 1980): 28–36.

Morris, William. "Art and Its Producers." In *William Morris on Art and Socialism*, pp. 208–19. Introduction by Holbrook Jackson. Paulton, Somerset, and London: John Lehmann Ltd., 1947. (III, IV)

_____. "The Aims of Art." In *William Morris on Art and Socialism*, pp. 82–95. Introduction by Holbrook Jackson. Paulton, Somerset, and London: John Lehmannn Ltd., 1947. (III, IV)

_____. "The Art of the People." In *William Morris on Art and Socialism*, pp. 38–56. Introduction by Holbrook Jackson. Paulton, Somerset, and London: John Lehmann Ltd., 1947. (III, IV)

_____. "The Beauty of Life." In *William Morris on Art and Socialism*, pp. 57–81. Introduction by Holbrook Jackson. Paulton, Somerset, and London: John Lehmann Ltd., 1947. (III, IV)

_____. "The Useful Work versus Useless Toil." *In William Morris on Art and Socialism*, pp. 175–93. Introduction by Holbrook Jackson. Paulton, Somerset, and London: John Lehmann Ltd., 1947. (III, IV)

_____. "The Lesser Arts." In *William Morris*, pp. 494–516. Edited by G. D. H. Cole. London: The Nonesuch Press, 1948.

_____. "Art and Labour" (1884). In *The Unpublished Lectures of William Morris*, pp. 94–118. Edited and compiled by Eugene D. Lemire. Detroit: Wayne State University Press, 1969.

Needleman, Carla. *The Work of Craft: An Inquiry into the Nature of Craft and Craftmanship*. New York: Alfred A. Knopf, 1979. (II)

Shahn, Ben. *The Shape of Content*. Cambridge, MA: Harvard University Press, 1957.

Snyder, Gary. *The Real Work: Interviews and Talks, 1964–1979*. Edited with introduction by William Scott McLean. New York: New Directions Publishing Corp., 1980. (II)

_____. *Axe Handles*. San Francisco: North Point Press, 1983.

Tobia, Blaise, and Maksymowicz, Virginia. "The Dilemma of Being Christian and Artist." *The Other Side* (December 1982): 16–18. (II)

Tyson, James L. "A Cathedral Grows in Manhattan." *The Christian Science Monitor*, August 1987, pp. 141–15.

Williams, Gerry, ed. *Apprenticeship in Craft*. Goffstown, NH: Daniel Clark Books, 1981. (I, II)

Yorke, Malcolm. *Eric Gill: Man of Flesh and Spirit*. New York: Universe Books, 1981.